LOVE
AND
HUNGER

LOVE
AND
HUNGER

CHARLOTTE
WOOD

ALLEN&UNWIN
SYDNEY·MELBOURNE·AUCKLAND·LONDON

First published in 2012

Allen & Unwin
Sydney, Melbourne, Auckland, London

83 Alexander Street
Crows Nest NSW 2065
Australia
Phone: (61 2) 8425 0100
Fax: (61 2) 9906 2218
Email: info@allenandunwin.com
Web: www.allenandunwin.com

Cataloguing-in-Publication details are available from the National Library of Australia

www.trove.nla.gov.au

ISBN 978 1 74237 776 6

Text design by Sandy Cull, gogoGingko
Set in 12.5/17 pt Granjon by Bookhouse, Sydney
Printed and bound in Australia by Griffin Press

10 9 8 7 6 5 4 3 2

*It seems to me that our three basic needs,
for food and security and love, are so mixed
and mingled and entwined that we cannot
straightly think of one without the others. So
it happens that when I write of hunger, I am
really writing about love and the hunger
for it, and warmth and the love of it and
the hunger for it . . . and then the warmth
and richness and fine reality of hunger
satisfied . . . and it is all one.*

MFK FISHER,
THE GASTRONOMICAL ME

CONTENTS

PART I
ORIGINS 1

PART II
PRACTICALITIES 55

PART III

OBSERVATIONS 135

PART IV

CONSOLATIONS 171

For my friends

PART I

ORIGINS

WHY COOK?

I began really learning to cook in my mid-twenties, at about the same time as I began really learning to write. I have only recently wondered if there is a link between these two things, other than the circumstances in which I found myself: an idle university student in possession of time for dawdling, some vague creative urges and new friends who inspired me with their own creativity and skill with a pen or a frying pan.

I had, of course, been cooking for years, in the way one does to feed oneself on first leaving home. I cooked sturdy, cheap and cheerful meals that were nutritious enough, if not exactly adventurous. I had also been writing for years, as a journalist on our small-town local newspaper, and I suspect the properties of my writing echoed those of my cooking. My articles—about artificial insemination of cattle, say, or the latest Lions Club fund-raising effort for a new piece of hospital equipment—were competent, and no doubt accurate enough. But the desire to write creatively, to bring out into the light and give shape and purpose to the inchoate longings and imaginings

3

of my young mind, was still too unformed—or else too deeply buried to acknowledge. I remember once being asked if I had ever thought about writing a novel. The idea seemed utterly ludicrous. My questioner might as well have asked if I had yearnings to captain a ship to Antarctica, or to become a world-famous belly-dancer. It was not just that such an achievement was beyond me, but I couldn't imagine why anyone would want to *expose* herself—to danger, to knowing—in such a way.

Skip a few decades to a recent dinner, when a dear friend who likes to be provocative suggested that people like me cook for others as a way of feeling superior to them. I admit I was a little rocked by this idea. Could he be right? Might there be even a kernel of truth in this? And if it wasn't true, why then do I cook, and why does the satisfaction it brings me feel so profound?

I hope my friend is wrong about my motives—or mostly wrong—but I do see his point, given the almost obscene contemporary obsession with what I think of as fashion cookery: the slavish reproduction of the latest television fad, the obedient queuing outside this cake shop or that restaurant, the cult-like allegiance to this brand of olive oil or that cookbook. All this worries me, because it seems born of a kind of competitive social anxiety rather than a confident love of food, and it makes cooking into a club of knowing insiders, excluding all others. The fetishisation of chefs and dishes and ingredients and equipment led one woman I know to declare in exasperation that she just didn't get this obsession with something as basic as food. 'I mean,' she cried, 'it's just *petrol*!'

I am not immune to food fashion, and some of it can be fun. But I aspire to something nearer to the ground, more elemental. The home cooks I know who have the most strongly anchored, easy relationship with their skill and interest in making food are somehow both serious and casual about it at once. They might make their own passata, but they would never dream of replicating an Adriano Zumbo cake. They spend hours a day reading food books, but couldn't give a damn about where 'the best' olive oil comes from.

But I'm drifting from the question. What is the nature of the pleasure I get from cooking?

Whenever we whined about being bored as children, our mother would call over her shoulder that we should 'go and do something constructive!'. This may well have sprung merely from the desire to get yet another of her five children out of her face for a moment, but she touched on something important: the deep fulfilment arising from the act of creating something that didn't exist before you made it. Whether it's a drawing, a paper plane, a garden bed or a tub of baba ghanoush—there is something fundamentally enriching about bringing something new into existence. It's constructive, in the most literal sense.

Another aspect of my pleasure in cooking is in the mental diversion it creates. When cooks speak of preparing a meal as a way of 'unwinding' or 'relaxing' after a hard day at work, I think there are several things at play. I am reminded of the great joy I felt for the year or so I went to Latin dancing classes. As with any kind of dancing involving patterns, what's essentially happening when you cook is a focused engagement with something physical and momentary, with patterns of repeated movements (chopping, stirring, turning a piece of fish or meat, for example). And in that focus on the physical, the mind may be freed from whatever had previously been occupying it. One woman I spoke to about this described it as 'free concentration'—a graceful transition from the intellectual part of her day to the leisure part of it. I wonder if this kind of freeing of the mind from niggling worries of the past hours or days or of future expectations, the intense focus and control only of the present moment, is part of the serenity that people seek from meditation.

At the same time as I am freed from the past and the future, though, in some subtle but definite way I am also connected, at least once every mealtime, to a cycle of life greater and more permanent than my own. This might sound grandiose, but pour a cupful of dried Puy lentils through your fingers and tell me you don't feel at least a faint twinge of earthy delight. Similarly, whenever I thump a cleaver through a piece of raw meat, it inevitably provokes a faint but definite stirring of some primal life-and-death struggle.

Pinching the bud of a basil flower off a knee-high plant by the kitchen door and tossing it into a pan of pasta sauce might not satisfy as deeply as making cheese from the milk of your own cows, as does one gentleman of my acquaintance, but it's still there, this tiny thread of connection between me and the earth. This thread is so fine nobody but me would notice it, and to others it may sound tenuous and highly romantic, but I don't care. It's true for me.

This kind of creativity is also mercifully free of public evaluation. In a creative field, your work is always attended by the possibility of humiliation—when a novel is published you are at the very least subject to several cool public assessments of your work, if not to newspaper declarations of your failure, or screeds of online comments about how stupid are your characters, how scant your ideas, how tedious your voice. Even when reviews turn out to be positive, the period of waiting for them makes opening the Saturday newspapers an exercise in nausea control for weeks, if not months, around publication time. So freedom from critical evaluation of the result makes the creative pleasure of cooking even deeper for me. Nobody is going to publicly declare your soufflé a workmanlike attempt in which the slight dip on the left-hand side ultimately led to the failure of the whole dish. For me, cooking (and gardening, a related pursuit) represents creativity in its purest form. It's no surprise that many fiction writers I know also have other private creative pursuits: one plays the ukulele, another sews stunningly beautiful bed quilts. We do these things partly, I think, because the strain of producing creative work under the watchful eye of reviewers, even publishers, even our beloved readers, can leach the work of much of its joy. It's work, after all. But cooking—or quilting, or ukulele-playing—is pleasure.

Ah, pleasure. Of course, physical pleasure must also be at the heart of every good cook's desire to do it. A friend (who, ironically, doesn't drink much at all) once told me she didn't trust teetotallers. To her, permanent abstinence from alcohol equates to a pathological fear of losing control, which in turn equals a fear of life. Having a couple of life-loving friends who don't drink at all, I'm not sure about that—but I certainly agree that a love of eating and drinking seem to correspond, among the people I know, with a love of life. A powerful appetite for food and an open emotional and intellectual appetite tend to go together—or perhaps that's my convenient prejudice.

What is not a prejudice but firm, proven data is something social researchers have been telling us for years: that connection with other people is what gives meaning and purpose to our lives. For me cooking creates the occasion and the place for those connections to happen. I remember several years ago stirring a pot of something in the kitchen, listening to the near-deafening hubbub of a dozen people sitting around the table in the next room, and thinking: I have never been happier in my life than in this moment.

But what about my devil's-advocate friend's assertion that people become good cooks in order to impress—even intimidate—others? Well, no doubt this is true for some. But I think the inverse is far more prevalent: that people become good cooks in order to be loved. The writer and former restaurateur Gay Bilson has spoken of her 'need to be needed' in this context, and in her book *Plenty* writes of the moment she learned, by making cream puffs for her family at age eleven, that cookery leads to praise. I think it would be a rare cook who could truthfully deny sharing these desires. For one thing, this kind of praise is so easy to get: any good cook will tell you that the compliments lavished upon them usually far exceed the effort it took to bring the lauded dish to the table. (This is not all sweetness and light, however; so bound up are my social life and my cooking that in my darker moments I have occasionally wondered whether, if I didn't make food for them, I would have any friends at all. If there is a sombre underside to be found in my cooking life, that is it.)

But some of the deepest satisfactions of cooking are not necessarily to do with sharing food with others, with the big dinner party or the impressive dish; it might be a single perfectly seared piece of salmon eaten on a weeknight in front of the television, or the pleasing consistency of a pea and mint soup eaten at your desk for lunch.

Thinking about the quiet but serious pleasure in these small moments, I finally recognise the most persistent feeling I have about my skill with cooking. It's not superiority, or even wantedness—it's that I feel lucky.

Every now and again someone will say to me wistfully, 'I wish I liked cooking.' I think my mother was probably this sort of person. My siblings may have differing opinions, but it seems to me she did not really like cooking much and yet she did it, hour upon hour, every day, with very little money, to provide nourishment for five children and a husband. Her garden was where her heart lay, and I think with a kind of sadness sometimes about how often she must have longed to be out in the garden instead of buttering yet another biscuit tray or chopping another carrot, and I blush at how much we complained about the food she so selflessly put on our table each night.

This is when I realise my luck. To derive so much pleasure from what to some people is a chore as joyless as vacuuming feels like an enormous stroke of good fortune.

Writing and cooking are, as I have said, two separate arenas of my life, and their separateness is part of what makes them both so satisfying to me—and yet here I am, bringing them together. But there is another thread that joins them. Like many before me,

I write fiction to find out what I think about the world; to open it up, look at it and place myself in it—and, in sending those books out into the public space, to share with others what I have found. In some ways, cooking does this for me too. When I try out a new technique or a recipe on my friends, or I pick a bay leaf from the little potted tree outside my kitchen, or I get excited by something as simple as a well-made frangipane tart, I am extending myself, discovering something new, and connecting myself to my world in a way that feels important.

As I write this I am increasingly impatient to get into the kitchen. I have ten people coming for dinner this evening, and I'm roasting two experimental chickens. I'm brining one of the birds before cooking, for the first time, to see why people make such a fuss about brining. As well, I've just been given a whole real truffle—an amazing black, chocolatey nugget of a thing—which I'm going to shave and put under the skin of the second chicken before roasting. I am more excited by these two experiments to come, and yet so anchored to my place in the world because of them, than it is possible to explain in words.

How to brine a chicken

Brining, a practice loved by Americans, is used to make roasted meats juicier, and can very subtly infuse the flesh with herbs and other flavours. This method is for brining a chicken of around 1.5 kg. I have tried it a few times, and found this method easy and very satisfactory, resulting in moist and delicately flavoured meat. One recipe I followed called for eight hours' brining, but the resulting meat was rather soggy and oversalted—I have found two hours the best length of time for a single chicken.

1 × 1.5 kg free-range or organic chicken

Handful thyme and rosemary sprigs

1 orange, cut into eight segments

1 lemon, quartered

1 teaspoon black peppercorns

3 fresh bay leaves

¾ cup salt

¼ cup sugar

1 cup hot water

3.5 litres water

1   Wash the bird and pat dry, then place in a large stock pot.

2   Add the thyme, rosemary, orange and lemon segments, peppercorns, and bay leaves to the pot.

3   In a separate saucepan, dissolve the salt and sugar in a cup of hot water over a low heat.

4   Add this to the 3.5 litres of cold water and pour over the chicken in the pot until you have covered the bird. (Use a plate to submerge it if necessary.)

5   Leave the chicken in the brine for around two hours, turning once. Remove the chicken, pat dry and roast as usual (see 'How to Roast a Chicken', page 107).

DISDAIN, REBELLION AND PORK BRAISED IN MILK: ON BECOMING AN ARTIST

Not long ago I read an article in the *Guardian* about the spiteful annotations made by Elizabeth David in the margins of other people's cookbooks. Unsurprisingly, David had a huge collection of food and recipe books, which were auctioned after her death in 1992. Now the Guildhall Library in London has collected, catalogued and archived the many personal notes she made on these books, scribbling them in margins, on the back of receipts, on scraps of paper and yellow post-it notes.

The remarks quoted in the newspaper—sharp, dismissive and imperious—made me feel even more warmly towards David than I did before. I have always liked prickly, opinionated people. And with contemporary cookery books so full of sappy emotion and syrupy language about hearts and hearths and helpings of love, it is a relief to read such simple, cranky declarations as *'This is NOT a tian'* and *'This is a useless book'* and even *'Waverley Root is a pitiful phoney'*.

I have an abiding love of Elizabeth David which is only tangentially to do with her cookbooks. The first time I ever heard of her was when I was invited to my painting and drawing teacher's house for a weekend lunch during my first year at university in Bathurst, New South Wales. My teacher and his spiky, intelligent and beautiful wife lived in a rambling old house in the village of Rockley, and when I walked through the front door, alive with excited nerves at being invited, I was met by an incredible smell. Something rich and garlicky was being slow-cooked in the kitchen, filling the house with its scent.

I was invited there, I think, because I had written a vignette about the studio where my teacher, David Wilson, had his art school. It wasn't a story, nor a poem, but a scrap, a few dreamy words. It was the first thing I had ever written that wasn't journalism. And, impelled by some fierce desire to be read, yet blushing with a furious embarrassment, I had thrust a folded copy of it into my teacher's hands after class one night. To my utter horror he began to read it there and then while I stood by, sick with shame. He read it, wiped his eyes, and told me it was beautiful. I couldn't speak. I bolted from the room. After that, whenever he introduced me to a fellow student or a life model or a visiting teacher (his friend John Olsen, on one occasion), David would say, 'Charlotte's a writer.' I blushed, the idea was still preposterous. But he planted a seed in my head; the seed of what I think of as a relaxed seriousness about art. The fact of being an artist was unremarkable—but respect for the *work* was everything.

A few weeks after he read my scrap of writing, David asked if I would join him, his wife Lu and a writer friend of theirs for lunch. When I think of how I must have looked that day—staring, mumbling, nodding, barely speaking—I recognise the silent, burning intensity I have seen in the faces of young women in writing classes ever since. The need to be recognised, and the gratitude—and fear—when it comes. For the three people at lunch that day spoke to me as a fellow artist, which shocked, thrilled and frightened me in equal measure. I looked at my plate, concentrating on the food. It seemed to me, sitting in that house full of Norman Lindsay paintings and art books and warm-toned, casually handled antiques, discussing art and books and the garden—where much of the lunch had come from—that this smell, this food, this way of eating was somehow a portal into an entirely new life for me, a simpler but richer mode of living than I had ever known existed.

It's not that my own upbringing was lacking in creativity—quite the opposite. I had a talented father who made half the furniture in the house as well as poetic, ethereal costumes for school plays, and from wire coathangers soldered teetering, intricate mazes for marbles for my brother. And my mother was a florist, so our house was always dotted with towers of striking beauty made of garden greenery, or smaller, surprisingly delicate arrangements that might appear on a windowsill. But food was never really a part of that creativity. Food, for my beleaguered mother, was a matter of filling up seven hungry stomachs every day in the most efficient and responsible manner possible before escaping out into her beloved garden. But the food I ate at David's and Lu's house that afternoon was, I intuited, somehow *to do with* art, not separate from it. It seemed to draw the very paintings from the walls, and the garden and the furniture and the conversation, into one living whole. In an unspoken and completely unpretentious way, it somehow fed not only the bodily but the creative selves of these people.

I think the dish that elegant Lu (who later became a friend too) cooked that day was *maiale al latte*—pork cooked in milk. It was delicious in an unearthly way. I had never eaten food like it. I remember the dish because I found the idea of cooking meat in milk completely astounding. When I asked her about it, Lu said it was 'just an old Elizabeth David thing'. Ah, I said, and nodded as if I knew what she was talking about. And noted the words *Elizabeth David, Elizabeth David* in my head.

Not long after, I came across my first copy of Elizabeth David's little Penguin paperback *A Book of Mediterranean Food* in a local op shop. It was destiny. I took the book home and began cooking *boeuf en daube à la niçoise* and *soupe au pistou* for my flatmates, and I began to fall in love with cooking.

I still have this book, even though the pages have fallen out and the cover is ragged. I bought a new hardback version a few years ago, but I kept the original one for sentimental reasons. Even though I only ever cooked a few things from it, this book seems deeply emblematic to me, in the way objects can so starkly represent those moments one has, as a young person, when you find a way of becoming your real self—I treasure it still for that reason.

I know there are plenty of Elizabeth David fetishists out there, and I suppose I may be one of them. I loved, for example, the television biopic *Elizabeth David: A life in recipes*, not because it was an accurate portrayal—which those who know their stuff about her tell me it absolutely wasn't, omitting any mention of her elite Tory childhood and patrician ways, for instance—but because it was a film about the creative struggle, and about abundance in the midst of post-war miserliness, and saying yes to personal freedom in spite of society's disapproval. And the price paid for all those things.

(As an aside, any novelist who has ever done a bookshop or library reading to an audience of four, two of whom are asleep and one of whom berates one for using, on page seventy-two, the word 'squashed' when he himself would have chosen 'crunched', should clasp to her bosom the scene in this film when cookery writer David goes to address a Women's Institute meeting. It is priceless.)

David's friend, the novelist Sybille Bedford, reportedly described her as 'very unforgiving, very temperamental, very severe in her standards', and others have painted her as a difficult snob. But I shall always be grateful for this very character, for that spirit of rebellion or snobbery (along with, doubtless, the Tory money) which sent her from England to the Continent, into and out of her miserable affairs and her drinking and her stroke. And I'll be grateful, too, for what many have seen as her unforgivable disdain for the lives of ordinary Britons, because a generation and a lot of geography later, it was that same rebellion and disdain that made an everlasting difference to my very ordinary life.

PORK BRAISED IN MILK

Adapted from an Elizabeth David recipe

Serves 6

Rolled loin of pork, about 1.2 kg

3 cloves garlic, sliced

2 sprigs rosemary

1 teaspoon coriander seeds, lightly crushed

1 teaspoon fennel seeds

2 tablespoons bacon, finely chopped

1 onion, finely chopped

Oil for frying

1 litre milk

Salt and pepper

1   If the pork is tied, unwrap it and remove the rind and most of the fat (don't worry, you won't lose any flavour!).

2   Place most of the garlic, 1 sprig of rosemary, most of the coriander and fennel and a pinch of salt in the centre, then roll up again and tie with kitchen string.

3   In a heavy-based casserole (best if it neatly fits the pork), brown the meat well on all sides in a little oil then remove from heat. Set meat aside and pour away the rendered fat.

4   Return the pan to the heat, add the bacon, onion and remaining herbs and garlic, and fry until soft in the residual fat from the meat.

5   Return the pork to the pot and pour in the milk—it should come about halfway up the sides of the meat.

6   Bring the milk to the boil for a few seconds and then turn down to a very gentle simmer. Keep the pan simmering on the stove top, partially covered and undisturbed, for about an hour.

7   After an hour, remove the lid. Hopefully the milk will have formed a skin—break it around the meat and scrape away from the sides of the pan. Continue to simmer uncovered for a further 30 to 60 minutes, until the meat juices run clear and the milk has formed clusters of pale golden curds. If you have a meat thermometer, check the temperature—it is cooked when the meat reaches 78°C. Once it is cooked, set meat aside in a warm place, loosely covered with foil, and continue to reduce the sauce if necessary until it thickens and forms buttery, oniony and bacony little nuggets which you can serve spooned over the sliced pork.

I serve this with green beans with a preserved lemon and garlic dressing (see page 276) and crisp roast potatoes.

A WOMAN OF STYLE, SUBSTANCE
AND HEDGEHOG SLICE

I have heard tonight that Mrs Spain, one of my mother's dearest friends, died this week. My mother died more than fifteen years ago, and I haven't really kept in touch with her friends. So it came as a great shock to hear that Marie, without question the most glamorous woman in my parents' country Catholic circle, was in her seventies (I realise I have always pictured her as still resolutely, elegantly forty-seven), had had Alzheimer's for some time, and in the past week apparently decided her time on earth was up, refused food and drink, and died quietly with her daughters by her side.

Marie Spain was quite a woman.

When we were small, our family of seven would turn up to Mass late every week, with each one of us kids looking as if we'd been torn through a bush backwards—hair fuzzed, clothes misbuttoned, faces unsuccessfully tissue-swabbed, still squirming and swatting at one another over some outrage committed in the kombi on the way to church. Once they had us safely captive in the pew, I think our exhausted parents must have closed their eyes with relief at the hour of enforced silence to come, for somehow the presence of God, incense and altar boys, combined with an icy parental stare when necessary, momentarily stilled the Beelzebubs within us.

Though we were always late, there was invariably one family who arrived later—but oh, so gratifyingly so. Each week, with a regal air I am certain they never knew they had, a procession of Spains would enter, all nine or twelve or sixty of them. (They had multitudes of children, plus various extraneous extended family members of all generations in constant residence, I seem to recall.) And they would take up their series of pews at the front of the church.

The differences between my family and the Spains were many and varied (mostly to do with sporting prowess, great warmth and good looks on their part, compared with wan, lank-haired spottiness and physical clumsiness on ours) but by far the most enthralling of these differences was that the Spains—every one of them, but none more than Marie—always dressed like a million bucks.

I don't think they had a million bucks, but Marie was one of those women of my mother's generation who could sew. I mean really sew, unlike our own efforts—the apologetic crookedly pinned, badly hemmed A-line skirts we would labour over under Mum's lacklustre supervision with the Singer threaded too tight. Marie's clothes were serious art: the kind of gorgeously French-seamed, satin-lined, magnificently tailored stuff women like me would now pay thousands for if we could afford it. But we never will, because that kind of skill and eye for beauty is almost lost, and therefore priceless.

Marie Spain arriving at Mass was something akin to Audrey Hepburn taking a stroll down the aisle of Our Lady Help of

Christians Church, Cooma North, every Sunday. She wore elaborate hats (which she made herself, of course) and, when called for, minxy black mantillas. She wore impeccably tailored suits in sumptuous fabrics, gleaming, unscuffed shoes with matching handbags, and fashionably brutal jewellery. This was the seventies: Marie wore fur, and tartan pantsuits, and slinky boots. In one glorious phase the Spains would come to church each week accompanied by a new movie-star mother in a fabulously funky wig: platinum bouffant one week, redhead flapper the next.

My sisters and I would gaze along the pews past our mother, past all the other perfectly presentable women like the ones we would grow up to be, who paled into insignificance beside Marie Spain. Hovering in her grotto on the wall above Marie, the boring old Virgin in her chipped blue plaster sack with her downcast eyes and her limp, defeated hair simply never stood a chance.

Marie and her husband Brian—a tall, strong, confident, handsome tennis champ with charisma to burn—made a dashing couple. It was as if a pair of birds of paradise landed on the church steps every week, a brood of chicks in training-plumage stepping along behind.

I'm told that the priest there now, a young chap, did not know Marie. It's almost unthinkable to me that her funeral might be presided over by someone who never witnessed this Sunday spectacular. But this is what I would like him to know: Marie was a woman of a steady, powerful gaze; slender shoulders; a firm handshake; perfect lipstick (red, I think); sleek, Twiggy-style haircuts; bold earrings; a husky, throaty, sexy laugh; a complete absence of bullshit; a conception of love and family (and God, I expect) that ignored all borders of blood or reasonable duty in order to embrace anyone having a moment of loneliness or need. She was woman of boundless love, enormous verve, enormous fun.

When our father became sick and died at fifty-three, Marie and Brian were always there for my mother, and for us. When our mother got sick a few years later, Marie and Brian were instantly by her side, full of love and outrage. When Brian, super-fit and indestructible, suddenly became ill himself and died devastatingly young, my family was shaken to the core for all the Spains. It was impossible that he had gone, and still feels like that. They were a team.

Tonight I feel the same all over again about Marie herself, though I haven't seen her for decades. I simply cannot shape my mind around the fact of her having grown old, being gone.

There is one more thing about her.

Every year on my father's birthday, Marie would show up at our house with a small plateful of her famous chocolate hedgehog slice. The stuff was legendary in our town. And in typically stylish fashion, Marie's hedgehog slice made an entrance: a few perfect squares artfully arranged on a white plate or wrapped in some elegant paper. It was always strictly for our father and him alone. The hedgehog slice would go straight into the fridge in its special wrapping until he came home from work. We kids were never allowed even to sniff it, though we stared longingly, holding the fridge door open, and I guess now and again we must have been given enough of a taste for me to have developed the Pavlovian response that still starts up whenever I recall it.

I think it took a woman with a hundred kids and endless demands upon her to understand something about the specialness of the biscuit equivalent of A Room of One's Own. How she managed it every year I don't know. But the hedgehog slice was our father's birthday treat, delivered by Marie every year without fanfare, without fail, and savoured every time.

So Vale Marie: fashion icon, generous soul, deeply loved woman with exactly the right overabundance of style and substance.

Marie's daughter Kate gave me her recipe for hedgehog slice after I made up my own in her memory. Here are both, in her honour.

MRS SPAIN'S HEDGEHOG SLICE

125 g butter

¼ cup sugar

1 tablespoon cocoa

1 teaspoon vanilla extract

1 egg, lightly beaten

1 cup coarsely crushed Marie biscuits (of course!)

1 cup walnuts

1 cup sultanas

Desiccated coconut, to sprinkle

1   Combine butter, sugar, cocoa and vanilla in a saucepan and stir over medium heat until dissolved and bubbling.

2   Remove from heat and allow to cool before adding egg. Mix well and heat again for a few minutes.

3   Remove from heat, add crushed biscuits, walnuts and sultanas, then push mixture into a loaf tin, sprinkle with coconut and refrigerate until firm.

4   Cut into squares, reserving five or six to take on a small plate to your friend on his birthday.

Homage hedgehog slice

My tribute version

250 g plain sweet biscuits (e.g. Milk Arrowroot)
¾ cup chopped hazelnuts
125 g butter
125 g sugar
2 tablespoons cocoa
2 tablespoons desiccated coconut
1 teaspoon vanilla extract
1 egg, lightly beaten
200 g good-quality dark chocolate

1   Crush biscuits, leaving some lumps. Place in a bowl with hazelnuts.
2   Combine butter, sugar, cocoa, coconut and vanilla in a saucepan over medium heat and stir until butter has melted.
3   Remove from heat and cool slightly, then add egg. Add to biscuit and nut mixture.
4   Melt chocolate and stir thoroughly into biscuit mixture.
5   Refrigerate until set, about an hour.
6   Cut into birthday squares, as above.

RECLAIMING THE HOSTESS GIFT

The mother of one of my friends has so deeply internalised the etiquette of never arriving at someone's house empty-handed that she even brings 'hostess gifts' when she comes to babysit, or pops in en route to the doctor—for any visit at all, in fact. It's an involuntary reflex, and her gifts have a legendary idiosyncrasy—a single green capsicum from the supermarket one day, a box of fish fingers or a package of toilet rolls the next. There may have been the occasional unkind family joke about these gifts, but nobody is in any doubt about the generosity and goodwill implicit each time.

I only learned of the term 'hostess gift' in recent years. My mother never used the expression, which to me evokes the women of Elizabeth Montgomery's *Bewitched*—all bouffant hair and ludicrous frilly aprons. But our mother did manage to instil in us the idea that turning up to someone's house for dinner empty-handed would be as vulgar as arriving only half-dressed. I understand such a gesture would be completely offensive in France, where it would imply some lack on the part of the host, but here in sunny Australia the convention is upheld by almost everyone I know, and I find it charming. Most common in our circle—and, let's face it, most obviously welcome—is the bottle or two of wine that everyone takes to any dinner at a private house.

But occasionally a friend brings something else instead. One of the great pleasures of having good cooks as friends is that when they come to your house for lunch or dinner they often bring with them a little morsel of some recipe they have been trying out. There is usually nothing outwardly impressive about these offerings, which are slung on to the kitchen bench or bunged in the fridge or decanted into a bowl there and then for tasting. They are wrapped in a bit of greaseproof paper, like Steph's jewel-like slabs of quince paste or her sticky salted caramels; or they might half fill a Vegemite jar, like Michelle's silky labneh in olive oil; or be wrapped in a cone of newspaper like the herb bouquet from Silas's garden; or drawn from a handbag on return from foraging, like Caro's jar of roasted cherry chutney from New Zealand or tube of umami paste from a posh deli in the city. Or the gift might simply be dumped in the sink in a plastic shopping bag, like the mixed harvest of beetroots and tomatoes and eggplants from Alice's garden. But sometimes they *are* beautifully presented, like the small but perfectly formed bulb of homegrown garlic presented by Dicky as a housewarming gift, wrapped in a little bridal muslin bag.

When my husband Sean and I are invited to visit these various friends, we briefly survey the fridge and the pantry for something to take along. Invariably there's a spare jar of chutney or marmalade or preserved lemon, or a fistful of herbs, a couple of tomatoes or some figs from a roadside stall, or a teeny near-failure of an eggplant from the garden.

A relative of the hostess gift is the occasion food present, like the ones my family give each other for Christmas. These gifts are rewarding because they are full of thought and effort and imagination. They often become traditions in themselves. If a Christmas went by without a box of my sister Bernadette's beloved mince pies, for example, Questions Would Be Asked. My sister Alice, a relaxed and practical person whom nobody would suspect of being a flower child, lately has taken her gifts to new earth-mothering heights; last year hers included not only a large jar of the lightest labneh I have ever tasted, but a bottle of her partner Simon's famous ginger beer, and another of elderflower cordial made *from flowers she grew herself.*

I find few things more pleasing than gifts like these. Beyond the obvious generosity—the sharing of the self in the effort of making or choosing or discovering or growing—they also have a kind of echo, in that the gift creates another: the dish cooked as a result, or the sharing or teaching of recipes and techniques that have become staples of my cooking repertoire. But there is also a playfulness and inventive pleasure in the reciprocal ritual of this exchange. The hostess-gift joke once took on epic proportions between Steph and myself as we exchanged back and forth—over about a year—the same jar of lurid vomit-yellow choko chutney she had purchased from Mr Nextdoor as a neighbourly courtesy. I believe she won when she left it on my doorstep, beautifully wrapped, as a birthday present.

I hereby declare it time to reclaim the hostess gift. The following are easy to make—so let's wrest the food gift away from frilly-aproned prissiness and give it back the earthy dignity it deserves.

POMEGRANATE HONEY

I learned of this heavenly nectar from the food blogs Kale for Sale and Nourish Me. It is a luscious drizzly syrup I use anywhere ordinary honey might be called for, or as a substitute for sugar.

1 pomegranate
1 jar clear honey (it doesn't work so well with crystallised
      honey)

1   Cut the pomegranate in half around its belly, cup a
     hand under the cut side of one half and smack the
     upturned side hard with a wooden spoon. The seeds
     should fall easily into your hand. Repeat with the
     other half.
2   Remove a few strips of pomegranate skin with
     a vegetable peeler, being careful not to take any
     white pith.
3   Add the seeds and skin to a jar of honey and set aside
     on a kitchen bench. If the weather is cool, leave the
     jar for a week or so before putting in the fridge. In

hot weather, a few days will do. Within a few days the honey will become a little runnier and gradually take on a pinkish hue.

4   Keep the honey in the fridge for as long as you like. I keep topping up the same jar with honey and pomegranate over the months. The more you use it, the more uses you will find: drizzle over yoghurt or ice cream, into salad dressings (especially good with bitter leaves like spinach or rocket), add to poaching liquid for fruit, and so on. A teaspoonful in a cup of hot water is also said to soothe a sore throat.

LABNEH

Makes around 3 medium takeaway containers' worth of labneh in oil.

1 kg full-cream Greek-style yoghurt
1 teaspoon salt
Olive oil
Dried herbs, chilli flakes, fresh garlic or rosemary

1   Line a colander with a good-sized piece of clean muslin—about 60 cm square or larger—and set it over a bowl (a fine linen tea towel would probably do as well, but would take rather longer).
2   Mix yoghurt and salt and pour it into the muslin.

3   Tie muslin corners together to make a bag of yoghurt.

4   Tie the muslin ends to a long wooden spoon handle and rest the spoon across the top of a deep cooking pot. Be sure to tie the muslin tight and hang it as high as possible, as it will lower over the hours. Mine has often eventually touched the bottom of the pot, necessitating retying halfway through. This is no big deal, though, and gives you a chance to pour out the whey—the cloudy liquid that drips out—if necessary.

5   Put the pot with the hanging yoghurt in the fridge for between 48 and 72 hours—the longer you leave it, the firmer the resulting cheese will be, but 48 hours results in soft but easy-to-form labneh.

6   Unwrap muslin and form labneh into balls (ping-pong-sized or smaller), keeping your hands moistened with olive oil to stop the labneh sticking to your hands and the balls to each other.

7   Lay the balls in a jar or container, cover with oil to which you have added some dried chilli flakes, dried herbs, fresh rosemary and a clove of garlic. (Any dried herbs would work.)

8   Use labneh as a spread or dip, on toast or a sandwich instead of butter, toss a ball into spicy soups or curries, add to steamed green vegetables or simply use anywhere you would add a dollop of yoghurt.

BABA GHANOUSH

The secret to good baba ghanoush is charring the eggplant skins first to get a good smoky flavour. If you don't have a barbecue they can be charred on the flame of a gas hob (be prepared for smoke) or simply roasted in the oven until very soft.

3 medium eggplants
2 tablespoons tahini
Juice of 1 lemon
1 large clove garlic
Salt
Olive oil
1 teaspoon ground cumin

1   Prick eggplants several times with a skewer, and then place whole on a barbecue, turning occasionally until the skins are deeply charred and the body yields very easily when prodded with tongs.

2   Remove from heat, split lengthwise to allow heat to escape, and leave to cool.

3   When cool enough to handle, scoop the eggplant flesh into a food processor. Don't worry if a few bits of charred skin go with the flesh—the result will be nicely smoky.

4　Add the tahini, lemon juice and garlic, and process very thoroughly till smooth. Add a little salt and taste. Add more salt, lemon or tahini, adjusting the flavour to your taste. Don't underseason.

5　While mixture is processing, add around half a cup of olive oil in a thin stream. Taste and add more oil if desired.

6　At the end add the cumin—grind the seeds yourself for an amazingly powerful flavour.

ALL THAT THE PALATE CRAVES:
THE LOVE OF LENTILS

'In good prose precision must always triumph over decoration,' writes the fictional novelist Logan Mount-Stewart in William Boyd's *Any Human Heart*. 'Wilful elaboration is a sign that the stylist has entered a decadent phase. You cannot live on caviar and *foie gras* every day: sometimes a plain dish of lentils is all that the palate craves, even if one insists that the lentils come from Puy.'

For some time now I have thought one of the things that separates real cooks from the rest is that real cooks love pulses. Pulses—lentils, chickpeas, dried beans and peas—are a kind of blank canvas, with which any reasonable cook can create a thing of wonder. But at the same time they have an honest beauty that, as Boyd suggests, can be enjoyed (almost) all on their own.

I came late to a love of lentils, but it is a love that has grown. It started with my discovery of exactly the pulse Boyd refers to above, the French Puy lentil—those small, beautiful beads which, just a few years ago, were only available in specialty shops. They're now so popular, especially as we are growing our own varieties in

Australia, that you can buy them alongside the split peas and 'soup mix' in the supermarket.

The Puy lentil—also known now as 'blue lentils' or 'French-style'—has several advantages over its Indian lentil or dried bean cousins. For one thing, it doesn't need soaking before cooking, unlike chickpeas or dried beans, and so can be flung into dishes at short notice. And it holds its shape beautifully—again, unlike other Asian or Indian lentils, which have their charms, but dissolve rather too readily to hold their own in other dishes.

But for me one of the greatest appeals of the French lentil is simply its striking beauty—to look at, to touch. I defy anyone to come across a bowl of these tiny blue-black river pebbles and resist the compulsion to run their fingers through them. As I write this, I have a small bowlful on the desk beside me, and have taken to idly dipping my fingers into the bowl as I think. Only just now have I realised that doing so recalls the loose, sensual pleasure I had as a child on illicitly riffling through the box of beads, jewels and earrings my mother kept in a wooden chest beside her bed. They make a lovely sound, too, like rain on a windowpane. There is something at once ancient and elegant about them.

Indeed, they are ancient. Archaeological evidence of lentils—a wild bush that was domesticated along with other crops such as barley and wheat—apparently dates back to the Palaeolithic and Mesolithic eras, and has been found in Greece, Syria and later around Jericho and Turkey. The crop was cultivated in Greece around 6000 BC, and Hippocrates is said to have prescribed lentils to his patients.

Lentils are even mentioned in the Old Testament, notably when Esau traded his birthright for bread and 'a pottage of lentils'.

At the beginning of the sixth century, the Byzantine Greek physician Anthimus, while serving as an ambassador to the king of the Franks, wrote a letter to him about good and bad foods titled *On the Observance of Foods*. It is considered the first French cookery book, and includes instructions for preparing the lentil soup known as 'puls'. The recipe still sounds rather good:

> *Lentils are good when washed and carefully boiled in fresh water. Make sure that the first lot of water is poured away, and a second lot of hot water added as required, but not too much, and then boil the lentils slowly on the hearth. When they are cooked, add for flavour a little vinegar, together with the addition of that spice which is called Syrian sumach. Sprinkle a spoonful of this spice over the lentils while they are still on the fire, and stir in well. Take the lentils off the fire and serve. You can for flavouring add a good spoonful of oil from unripe olives to the second lot of water while the lentils are still cooking, as well as one or two spoonfuls of coriander including the roots— not ground but whole—and a pinch of salt for seasoning.*

Anthimus would have been pleased to see his belief in the health-giving benefits of lentils supported by a 2004 study published in the *Asia Pacific Journal of Clinical Nutrition,* which points out that a diet high in legumes is 'the most protective dietary predictor of survival amongst the elderly, regardless of their ethnicity'. This same study reports that 'the significance of legumes persisted even after controlling for age at enrolment (in 5-year intervals), gender, and smoking. Legumes have been associated with long-lived food cultures such as the Japanese (soy, tofu, natto, miso), the Swedes (brown beans, peas), and the Mediterranean people (lentils, chickpeas, white beans).'

The first time I cooked Puy lentils was in a recipe for salmon wrapped in pancetta, served on a bed of lentils, spinach and spiced yoghurt. I had to cross town to find the lentils, and they were devilishly expensive, but once I found them I vowed never to let them go. They held their shape so beautifully, and they had a nutty, earthy flavour I found I loved.

Until then, I had thought I disliked lentils. And I did—or at least the ones I had tasted in the powdery, unseasoned, gluey bowls of tasteless gloop served up in share houses the nation over by me and my fellow youthful cooks. Dishes such as those led to the lentil being maligned as 'hippie food', even now, among people who should know better. (The food writer AA Gill springs to mind, telling a Sydney Writers' Festival audience that he once sent back a dish at a friend's dinner party. It was, he claimed in a voice dripping with revulsion, 'lentil *bake*'. And when a *MasterChef* contestant turned up her nose at lentils as 'beige food' a couple of years ago, I knew she was not my kind of cook.)

Of course it is ignorant to revile the lentil these days, but a few decades ago in Australia things were different.

After my friend Fenella lost her mother at sixteen, she took on all the cooking for her brother and father. In her early teens she had begun to learn sophisticated French cookery, working from the *Cordon Bleu* magazines her mother ordered for her every week from the newsagent, but by the time her mother died Fenella had become a health-conscious vegetarian with, she says, a rather limited culinary vocabulary.

'I have such a vivid memory of my poor father, night after night, valiantly making his way through bowls of watery curried dhal made from red lentils atop brown rice, and without a word of complaint. Every time I eat curried red lentils I'm taken straight back to those nights, sad and lonely with just the three of us all of a sudden and this rather miserable, if nourishing, meal.'

In an award-winning magazine feature, 'A Voyage Around My Kitchen', Fenella related her discovery of good cooking at seventeen, through her French boyfriend. Or more accurately, and far more importantly, through his mother, 'a terrifying matriarch Balzac might have created'. The mother never smiled, and was cool, to say the least, towards Fenella. But . . .

> *Whatever the time of day, there was always something good to eat. A cruet of olive oil and vinegar lived on the table. A simple lentil salad, with Puy lentils (heaven knows how Mrs P got hold of them back then—she might have had a relative send them over) might appear, tangy with lemon juice, beside a plate of pillowy sautéed leeks. There was always a green salad, but made with leaves I'd never seen, frozen as we were in Australia's iceberg years.*

It was by observing how the terrifying Mrs P handled vegetables that Fenella gained entry to a whole new world of pleasure in food and its preparation. I feel the little Puy lentil led me, eventually, to the same world. It somehow symbolises a way of cooking vegetables with ease and simplicity and a delight in texture and colour and flavour, with none of the forlorn drabness that was part of the DNA of all those student-digs bowls of curried slop with their raw spices and underseasoning.

So it was the French lentil that would change my attitude not only to lentils in general (and eventually even lead to my veneration of a good dhal with its comforting velvety warmth and subtle, layered spicing), but also make me look again at and seek out all the other pulses—the split peas, the now beloved chickpea and all manner of dried beans—that I had hitherto disparaged. And I have become something of an evangelist for the humble lentil—too beautiful, too luxurious, to remain captive in the miserably nourishing health-food aisle.

SIMPLE BRAISED LENTILS
Serves 2

1 stick celery, finely chopped

1 carrot, finely chopped

3 cloves garlic, finely chopped

Half small fennel bulb, finely chopped

2 rashers bacon or equivalent speck or pancetta, finely
    chopped

Olive oil

1 cup dried Puy lentils

1 fresh bay leaf, torn

5 sprigs thyme

1 litre chicken or vegetable stock

1 ripe tomato, finely chopped

Salt and pepper

½ bunch parsley, chopped

1   Sauté celery, carrot, garlic, fennel and bacon in a good
    lug of olive oil until soft and bacon has begun to brown.

2   Add lentils, bay leaf and thyme, stir until well coated
    with oil and fry for 1 minute.

3   Add stock and tomato, bring to the boil and then
    reduce heat to simmer gently, covered, for around

20 minutes or until the lentils are tender but holding their shape.

4 Remove cover and gently reduce the liquid until the mix is loose and soft. If it gets too dry and stodgy, add hot water a little at a time.

5 Season to taste, stir in parsley and a slosh of olive oil, then serve as a side dish or bed under fish, chicken or roast meat.

LENTIL, SUN-DRIED TOMATO AND PARSLEY SALAD

1 × 400 g can lentils
½ cup sun-dried tomatoes, plumped in hot water, roughly
    chopped
⅓ bunch parsley, finely chopped
1 tablespoon balsamic vinegar
Salt and pepper
Olive oil

1 Drain and thoroughly rinse the lentils. Place in a bowl.
2 Add tomatoes, parsley, vinegar and seasoning.
3 Add a slosh of olive oil to add gloss and flavour. Check all seasoning and adjust vinegar to taste.

GREEN SALAD WITH LENTILS AND GOAT'S CHEESE

½ cup Puy lentils

2 cups vegetable or chicken stock

2 cups mixed salad leaves (include some springy ones such
   as curly endive or radicchio if possible)

2 fresh or slow-roasted tomatoes, cut into pieces

3 tablespoons good olive oil

1 tablespoon balsamic vinegar

Salt and pepper

250 g marinated goat's cheese or a few balls of labneh
   (see page 31)

1   Combine the lentils and stock in a saucepan and
     simmer for 20 minutes or until tender. Drain and
     return the lentils to the pan with a splash of olive oil
     until ready to assemble salad.

2   Toss the lentils with salad leaves and tomatoes in
     a bowl.

3   Combine the oil and vinegar, season well and dress
     the salad.

4   Tear the goat's cheese or labneh into shreds the size of
     20-cent pieces and toss them through the salad.

LENTILS AND RICE

Serves 2

¼ cup wild rice

½ cup Basmati rice

¼ cup Persian red lentils

¼ cup currants soaked in red wine vinegar

1 onion, sliced and fried until very crisp and dark

1 tablespoon mint leaves, torn

Salt and pepper

1   Cook the rice and lentils in three separate pots of boiling water until tender (the wild rice will take up to 45 minutes), then drain and mix.

2   Stir through the currants, onion and mint, check seasoning and serve.

SEE ALSO

Spinach dhal (see page 79).

ROADSIDE ASSISTANCE

🍎

Sometimes it's easy to feel swamped by the grime and aggression of urban life.

I love living where we do, in the inner west of Sydney. But occasionally I am overwhelmed by the barrage of noise from cars, leaf blowers, garbage trucks, street sweepers and aircraft. And living only a few hundred metres from an ageing, mid-sized shopping mall, we are also quite often treated to less-than-charming episodes of human behaviour floating in through our open windows as people pass to and fro. Add this to all the other urban intrusions on one's mental space, and there are days when city living simply becomes too much.

Happily, this urban stress syndrome (I believe this is now an officially designated ailment) can be quickly alleviated by a drive into the country, like the night we spent late last summer with friends at a house on the Hawkesbury River, about an hour and a half from home. Sitting on the veranda of that house early on Saturday morning, watching the river glide silently by, was the most restorative tranquilliser I could have wished for at the end of a long and noisy week.

And even though we couldn't stay long, the drive home was just as recuperative as the night away. This time, instead of flying past in a hurry as we too often do when returning from the country, we decided to take the trip slowly and stop at many of the roadside food stalls along the way. After that weekend I decided to do this every time we leave the city—because as well as filling your fridge or your fruit bowl, there's something satisfying about buying food in this way. It's to do with bringing a little of the landscape home with you, and with closing the gap between you and where your food comes from. Even if the produce is bought from a van parked on the side of the road rather than the farm itself, the person selling it to you has usually either grown it themselves or knows the person who did. There's a human connection in this passing of food from their hands to yours that I find very soothing. It generally means you're eating seasonal food, too—most roadside stalls appear when there's a glut—which promotes a direct connection to the earth and the weather. This is a welcome contrast to grocery shopping in the city; even if you avoid the worst supermarkets it can tend to make you feel like a cog in a great big industrial food machine. And last, there's the aesthetic enjoyment, as many of the jerry-built wooden stalls and hand-painted signs—quite apart from the pleasing arrangements of the food itself—have a rough-hewn, purely utilitarian beauty. On our drive home from the river that day we stopped at a farm-gate stall made from wood and corrugated iron, shading cartons of fresh eggs (the chooks were visible not far down the hill), some capsicums in a box and bags of green beans and beautifully ripe Roma tomatoes. Prices were written in felt pen on a torn piece of cardboard, and by a coffee jar with a lid sat another handwritten sign, this one on a piece of wood: PLEASE LEAVE MOAD IN JAR. We had no idea what it meant, but left our payment there. (My canny sister-in-law later told me MOAD means 'money or a donation'.)

The seasonal aspect of this kind of food shopping tends to rejuvenate one's cooking, too, as what you buy dictates what you eat for the next little while, and coming up with different ways to cook the same ingredient can nudge one out of a rut. By the time we made it home from the Hawkesbury that day we had stopped a couple more times, once to buy a kilo of fresh 'bulotti' beans from an Italian gent with a white van parked on the roadside, and two kilos of ripe figs from a demountable shed outside a farmhouse.

For two people to work their way through two kilos of figs in the short time before they would over-ripen required a little imagination, so that week became a festival of the fig in our house. Apart from the usual fig halves wrapped in prosciutto as a snack, we made a dessert of figs with spiced labneh, and adapted a Maggie Beer recipe for spatchcock 'in a fig bath', replacing the bird with a succulent piece of quickly roasted pork fillet. I threw some of the remaining figs into a salad inspired by a luscious one I ate at my friend Leslie's house, and used the rest in a very simple fig preserve to eat with blue cheese. The tomatoes were easily dealt with; as I slow-roasted half to keep in oil in the fridge and use in everything from salads to sandwiches or stirred through pasta, puréed another six or so to throw into a fish curry, and had a big bowl left for salads. Half the fresh borlotti beans went into a salad, and half into Boston baked beans. And each time we ate one of these dishes, we heard a faint but lovely echo of the river lapping at the edges of the lawn.

LESLIE'S LUSCIOUS FIG SALAD
Serves 6

About 9 fresh figs
Olive oil
4–5 slices prosciutto, torn
¼ cup balsamic vinegar
1–2 tablespoons brown sugar
Handful radicchio leaves
Handful basil leaves
3 tablespoons marinated feta cubes
Salt and pepper

1   Cut figs into halves or quarters and brush with a little olive oil. Grill these on a tray with the prosciutto for a few minutes until the figs are warmed and the prosciutto crisp.

2   Meanwhile, simmer the balsamic vinegar and sugar in the smallest pan you have, and gently reduce until thick and syrupy.

3 Arrange radicchio leaves in a bowl (or, more glamorously, on separate plates for each person) and drizzle with good olive oil.

4 Top with the figs and prosciutto and add feta cubes.

5 Gently mix these and the leaves together with clean hands, then add the basil leaves.

6 Drizzle the balsamic syrup over and season.

FRESH FIGS WITH SOFT LABNEH

Figs—I use 2 per person
500 g Greek-style yoghurt
50 g brown sugar
¼ teaspoon ground cardamom
A few saffron threads
¼ cup pistachio nuts, chopped
Pomegranate honey (see page 30), or ordinary honey

1 Make labneh, following method on page 31, but omitting salt and stopping before step 5.

2 Remove labneh from muslin, whisk in sugar, cardamom and saffron, and chill for at least 1 hour.

3 Serve figs in shallow dessert bowls topped with the spiced labneh and nuts and drizzled generously with pomegranate honey.

SLOW-ROASTED TOMATOES

Roma tomatoes
Sea salt
Pinch caster sugar
Olive oil
Handful thyme sprigs

1   Preheat oven to 150°C.
2   Halve the tomatoes lengthwise, place on an oven tray, and sprinkle the cut sides with salt and a tiny pinch of caster sugar.
3   Drizzle with olive oil.
4   Roast in the oven for a few hours until they are as caramelised as you like them.
5   Keep in the fridge covered in oil, for use in salads, on toast, tossed through pasta or anywhere you would use canned tomatoes, for a slightly deeper flavour.

BOSTON BAKED BEANS

Serves 4

500 g podded fresh borlotti beans (or dried white beans, soaked overnight and rinsed)
2 tablespoons Dijon mustard

2 tablespoons maple syrup

1 tablespoon honey

4 cloves

1 large onion, halved

100 g smoky bacon, chopped

2 fresh bay leaves

Oil

1 × 400 g can tomatoes

¼ cup red wine vinegar

Salt and pepper

1   Place the beans in a heavy-based pan, cover with water and slowly bring to the boil. Simmer gently over low heat for 15 minutes (fresh borlottis) or about 30 minutes (dried beans), until half-cooked. Drain.

2   Preheat oven to 140°C.

3   In a bowl combine the mustard, honey and maple syrup.

4   Insert 1 clove into each onion half, then toss over a high heat for a few minutes in a large, ovenproof casserole with the bacon, remaining cloves, bay leaves and a splash of oil.

5   Add tomatoes, beans and the mustard mixture, stir well and cover.

6   Bake in the oven for anything up to 4 hours, checking every 30 minutes or so to see how tender the beans are, adding water if it gets too dry.

7   For the last half-hour, remove the lid, add the vinegar and cook uncovered.

8   When the beans are as tender as you like them, check seasoning—adjusting the sweetness to taste—and serve.

FRESH BORLOTTI BEAN SALAD

1 kg fresh borlotti beans
4 tablespoons chopped bacon or pancetta
Handful parsley, finely chopped
1 clove garlic, finely chopped
Good-quality olive oil
Sea salt and pepper
Juice of ½ lemon

1   Pod the borlottis from their slinky pink sleeves, toss them into boiling water for 10–20 minutes or until just tender, then drain.

2   Fry the bacon or pancetta in a hot pan, then turn off the heat.

3   While beans are still hot, bash them about a little with a wooden spoon, then add to the pan with the bacon.

4   Add parsley and garlic and stir to combine.

5   Put the beans in a bowl and toss with a generous
    slurp of olive oil, a pinch of sea salt, pepper and lemon
    juice to taste.

VEGETARIAN OPTION

Omit bacon.

PART II

PRACTICALITIES

THE JOY OF COMPETENCE

Why is the mastery of basic skills in the kitchen so satisfying— and, conversely, why does lack of expertise in supposedly simple techniques such as chopping an onion, say, or carving a chicken or separating an egg, feel so dispiriting?

The discovery of ease—even pleasure—in an otherwise irritating task makes it more enjoyable. When I finally learned how to chop an onion without tears, for example, I was elated—but it wasn't only my dry eyes that pleased me. It had something to do with finding enjoyment in an aspect of cooking I had always hated, and it is evidence that a mastered skill—or competence, as the scholar and food writer Tammi Jonas has written—equates with pleasure.

I must have learned a few basic skills in the dreary cooking or 'home economics' classes we endured at school, but I remember very few. I hated Home Ec, as we called it. Even the name implied deprivation, dullness and sobriety. As an adult I have wondered if my feelings might have been different had the classes been called Making Feasts, or How to Have a Party.

In my memory of Home Ec there was always more emphasis on perfectly ironed napkins and aprons and the folding of tea towels, on being *neat*, than the actual taste or aesthetic appeal of anything we cooked. And all the food was white: eggs, junket, porridge, suet, mashed potato. It was the cusp of the 1980s when I trudged into the classroom for these things, but it felt like 1949.

I used to think it must have been my imagination that exaggerated the cheerlessness of Home Ec, but at a garage sale recently I found an illustrated copy of our Home Ec bible, *The Commonsense Cookery Book*, and I see my memory serves me surprisingly well. When I realise just exactly how disgusting was the food we were learning to cook, it's no wonder I hated it. In the copy of this book I have beside me, published in 1976, there are recipes for more than 130 savoury dishes. Only three include garlic: Spaghetti Bolognese, which calls for 'three thin slices of garlic', Minestrone Soup, and Chicken and Almonds, each of which uses 'one small clove'. The only fresh herb I can find in the whole book is a sprig of parsley—curly, of course. And this, I remind you, was more than twenty years after Elizabeth David first began publishing her books on Mediterranean and French country cooking.

The recipe names seem to compete in their joylessness . . . Fried Sausages. Dry Curry. Eggless Pudding. It's as if the whole book is stuck in a mindset of post-war rationing, and even the pleasure that might arise from a profligate use of words is frowned upon. What else can explain Economical Batter? There is something called Sea Pie, which contains nothing from the ocean but does include sheep's kidneys and turnip. There is a thick sauce (white, naturally) known alarmingly as Masking Sauce.

There is a whole chapter titled 'Dishes Suitable for Convalescents, the Aged, and Children'—just the heart's desire for any fourteen-year-old girl bursting with life and youth and beauty. Arrowroot gruel or brain cakes, anyone?

I know it's probably unfair of me to take aim specifically at this book, when doubtless it was just an expression of the broader culture. But I feel a strange residual anger when I look at it, for it seems *so* petty, *so* miserly in spirit, and such a stark symbol of what the lives of women were about (there were no boys in my cooking classes—they got to do woodwork). This was what Home Ec was preparing us for: cheerless kitchen servitude. Domestic drudgery devoid of any of the pleasure or creativity I was later to find so essentially satisfying. I still feel ripped off—as perhaps do some of those boys who would have loved nothing more than to stop banging nails into wood and start banging around with pots and pans instead.

However, I do recall one single moment of pure satisfaction during a Home Ec class: when I learned that if you shake the mixing bowl while rubbing butter into flour, the big lumps rise to the top. How simple—and how ingenious—a solution to rummaging about in the bowl for the bits of butter yet to be rubbed.

(I got terrible marks for all my dishes, by the way—my cakes were always too flat and my poached eggs too waterlogged, or too hard, or too something. Earlier than this, I had also failed in my attempt to earn the Cooking Badge in Brownies by boiling dry a pot of frozen peas and scorching the saucepan.)

The first basic kitchen skill I was shown as an adult was chopping garlic, using that rapid rocking motion and the curled-under fingers of your other hand as a guide. My teacher was my friend Ali, a fellow uni student who had worked in restaurants and knew a thing or two about cooking. She was one of the people who planted the seed of love for cooking in my life. Her meals were unfussy, always perfectly cooked and, importantly, beautifully presented. I remember once visiting her house, full of the fifties op-shop furniture we all loved, and she cooked me dinner of loin chops and vegetables. Instead of apportioning the food in the kitchen, Ali put everything on one large platter from which we served ourselves sitting on the living room floor and eating at the coffee table. It was such a simple thing, but in those days before television cooking shows and magazines and the elevation of food 'styling' to a commercialised art, this was one of my first lessons in cooking and aesthetics, about the generosity implicit in making a meal *look* attractive and bounteous, no matter how plain the food itself might be.

Once I mastered the chopping, I was hooked on the pleasure of basic techniques mastered. I think this is one of the things that enthusiastic amateur cooks most love to share and learn from one another. That said, I love a professional lesson as much as the next person and having a respected restaurant chef for a brother-in-law has given me previously-undreamed-of access to lessons in techniques as satisfying as boning and trussing a chicken (we practised the latter on a tissue box; highly recommended).

The internet has brought new access to good culinary techniques. I love that there is not a skill you can't find on video by typing 'how to . . .' into a search engine. It's here I finally discovered the easiest way to carve a roast chicken, and perfected my onion-chopping technique. And one of the most enjoyable dinners I've cooked for friends included my first-ever attempt at soufflé, from a video on the internet. Dessert time involved the whole eight of us crowded round the laptop in the kitchen, one person shouting instructions at me as I folded in the egg whites in loops, another passing the ramekins, and the whole crowd cheering when the soufflés emerged, some slightly lopsided, from the oven. We diagnosed the flaws together—too runny inside, not enough greasing of the ramekin edges on a couple—but savoured them nonetheless.

All good cooks like to watch others working in the kitchen, I think, and the sharing of technique is as important a part of their cookery friendships as shared recipes. This is how I learned from my friend Caro that chopping herbs can be as easily done with scissors in a cup, or from my sister, decades ago, that a roux is ready for milk when it moves easily away from the edges of a pan.

My friend Hannie tells of her first days as a waitress in the 1970s, when the 'handsome and dangerous Spanish chef' asked her if she liked garlic. She replied yes, of course, hoping for some flirtatious sippings from spoons or popping of morsels into mouths, but instead he dumped a shopping basket of garlic cloves on the bench and said, 'Good. Peel these!'

'I began peeling slavishly,' she recalls, 'snipping the top off the garlic and pulling down each skin. He let me do this for some time, then sighed, pushed me aside and banged the lot with a meat cleaver. All the skins fell off.'

We all know how to do this now, but happening as it did during Australia's dreary *Commonsense* years, I can just imagine Hannie's thrill at the earthy magicianship of such a gesture. In fact, I think this is one of the deep pleasures of a basic skill mastered—the obvious simplicity of it suddenly revealed; the almost magical conversion of a tedious chore into a kind of art. It may sound ridiculous to take such delight in the chopping of an onion, but this transformation of work into pleasure still surprises me, and is one of the real delights of cooking.

HOW TO CHOP AN ONION

I used to *hate* chopping onions—my eyes would sting and stream so uncontrollably I could barely see, and the result was not small neat dice but lumpish shards and strips, as if I had bludgeoned the thing into submission rather than firmly taken charge of it. After some research and talking with my cooking friends, including my dear chef brother-in-law Hamish, whose first recommendation was to practise on twenty kilos of onions (his second was to make an apprentice do it), I have come up with the following tips.

Chill your onions first   I know, they are rumoured to emit gases and make other vegetables age more quickly, but I am now convinced a colder onion creates fewer tears. Restaurants keep theirs peeled *and* chilled, and I'd take the risk of a slightly softer neighbouring eggplant over tearful agony and a badly chopped onion any day. I keep at least two onions (skins on) in the fridge at all times, and sometimes toss one in the freezer for fifteen minutes if necessary.

Sharpen your knife   This goes for everything, of course, but especially onions. A clean cut means less vapour.

Keep a damp cloth handy   Wipe the surface of your board frequently during chopping and there will be less juice to cause you pain.

Now to the chopping

1. Cut the onion in half lengthwise, retaining a portion of the root on each half. This is important, as it will hold the onion together as you slice.
2. With the cut side flat to the board, make multiple, evenly spaced cuts longways from the root to the outer edge, using the curled fingers of your other hand as a moving guide as you cut. *Do not cut through the root end*—this way the onion will hold together, and fewer vapours will escape.
3. Make two horizontal (or slightly angled) cuts into your onion from the now 'tasselled' edge, reaching almost, but not quite, to the root end.
4. Holding the onion together with your free hand, simply slice as if you were making onion rings. Pushing the knife forward rather than straight down will allow it to do its work more easily. When you are done, scrape the onion away, wipe the board and begin again with the other half.

At the end of this you should have a little heap of fairly uniform onion dice, few tears and a nice sense of satisfaction. The more you practise, the better you get, and the easier—and more pleasurable—it is.

AN EXPRESSION OF CIVILISED
CUISINE: HOW TO BE A HOST

'I have heard of people's lives being changed by a dramatic or traumatic event—a death, a divorce, a winning lottery ticket, a failed exam. I never heard of anybody's life but ours being changed by a dinner party.'

So wrote Wallace Stegner in one of my favourite novels, *Crossing to Safety*, a tender portrayal of a lifelong, deep and sometimes difficult friendship between two couples. The friendship begins when the Langs invite the Morgans to dinner:

> When the Langs opened their house and their hearts to us, we crept gratefully in.
>
> Crept? Rushed. Coming from meagerness and low expectation, we felt their friendship as freezing travelers feel a dry room and a fire. Crowded *in*, rubbing our hands with satisfaction, and were never the same thereafter. Thought better of ourselves, thought better of the world.

*In its details, that dinner party was not greatly different
from hundreds we have enjoyed since. We drank, largely and
with a recklessness born of inexperience. We ate, and well, but
who remembers what? Chicken Kiev, saltimbocca, escallope
de veau, whatever it was, it was the expression of a civilized
cuisine, as far above our usual fare as manna is above a baked
potato. A pretty table was part of it, too—flowers, wine in
fragile glasses, silver whose weight was a satisfaction in the
hand. But the heart of it was the two people who had prepared
the occasion, apparently just to show their enthusiasm for Sally
and me.*

I have certainly had this feeling—that my life has been changed
by a dinner—more than once, and I would like to think it has
occasionally happened for others at our house. If my friends are to
remember me for anything when I'm gone, I would like it to be
for the gatherings around our table. For Stegner makes clear here
what I have always felt: that gathering people in your house, around
your table—sharing your food and your company with a generous
spirit—is not trivial.

The most significant thing about the excerpt above, of course, is
that the food is far less important than the welcome and the warmth.
Or perhaps more accurately, the food is symbolic of those things, is
a part of them, rather than something separate.

So how does this happen, exactly? What is it that lifts dinner
out of the ordinary into the realm that Stegner describes? I gathered
some of the most gracious hosts I know to lunch at my house

recently to discuss this. I asked them what the responsibilities of the host might be, and how these should be discharged. And what about the guest—does she have her own obligations, beyond turning up?

Almost as soon as my friends arrive they begin arguing against the term 'dinner party' itself—and there is unanimous, almost instant, agreement that the term should be banned. It reminded some people of occasions hosted by their parents which—while often starring excellent food—seemed in memory to have a starched, uptight feeling about them. My own childhood memories of dinner parties are more exciting. My parents gave dinner parties only rarely; I don't recall much about the food, but as children we loved setting the proper dining table—the large mahogany drop-sided one in the living room, as opposed to the little pine one we squashed around in the kitchen for our nightly meals (the former was a beautiful table, even after my sister Alice scratched her name with a Stanley knife into its one fat pedestal base—I wonder if the thieves who eventually stole it from my mother's house ever removed that scratched signature, or if it lives on, in another dining room somewhere . . .). There were ironed napkins and little bowls of peanuts and the good bone-handled cutlery, and although we were sent to bed almost as soon as the guests arrived, we spent a lot of time creeping down the hallway and sitting in the dark to listen to the gaiety beyond.

But that was a long time ago, and while 'dinner party' may have been an apt description for occasions at both the Langs' in 1940s America and at my parents' fibro bungalow in 1970s Cooma

North, my friends are adamant that the term is out. Too stiff, too intimidating, they say. Creates too much expectation. 'Come to dinner,' is the invitation they issue most often, and most like to receive.

So perhaps this is where it begins, the feeling of warmth and joy that Stegner evokes—with the tone of the invitation. These days my entire social life is organised by email, and there's nothing remotely formal about it. It's just a setting of dates, really. But when I think about the dinner invitations I receive, whether by email or phone or text message or gilt-edged parchment (okay, so I've never actually had one of those), I realise that those I most look forward to somehow, from the very beginning, have this sense of ease and generosity.

Ease. This is a word that keeps arising during the hours of our talking, and it becomes clear that no matter how much effort goes into the preparation of the food and the table—which can often be a great deal—there must be no evidence of that effort on the night. A novelist friend, Tegan, is reminded of Annie Dillard's injunction in *The Writing Life* that the effort of the writing must not be visible in the work. 'Process is nothing: erase your tracks.'

Several behind-the-scenes things help to create this ease, we decide. First, preparing as much of the food as possible ahead of time most definitely helps, as does cooking a meal that you know is basically within your capability. My friend Rachel explains why this matters. Her friend Deb, who lives alone, occasionally invites Rachel and others over for dinner. They feel tense as soon as the invitation is given, because they know they can expect an ordeal. For some reason, Deb feels compelled to cook alarmingly complicated food, which usually demands a level of skill beyond what is comfortable for her.

'Because she's never done it before her timing is way out,' says Rachel. 'So when we ring the doorbell she greets us sweaty, stressed, a bit drunk, and already cranky with us for being the cause of all this drama. Once inside, you're given some stressful job to do—timing the fish, or reading out some incomprehensible cheffy recipe, or washing the glassware, which is very precious so you better not break it. By the time you get to eat—late—everybody is too drunk to be hungry, the food is no good, under- or overcooked or otherwise ruined because nobody knew how to cook it, there's no conversation because everyone is so anxious and uptight, and you all walk out thinking that was the worst night of your life. Then you realise that Deb is still there—angry, alone, and faced with a mountain of washing-up, and you feel guilty and upset about the whole thing.'

I feel quite tense just listening to this report, which evokes layers of sadness and dissatisfaction that, while manifested in the dinner, are about so much more: loneliness, anxiety to impress, and resentment—the occasion could be so different if Deb herself could be satisfied with perfecting a bowl of pasta and pouring everyone a glass of good wine. It reminds me of the relief when I learned years ago, from the example set by my friend Peter, that a single course, perfectly cooked and presented with relaxed goodwill, is far more debonair than all the fiddly starters and fancy desserts in the world. And now I recall the sane words of Dr Edouard de Pomiane, mid-twentieth-century French culinary chemist and provocateur, who advises this on the duties of a host: 'One should prepare only one good dish. This should be preceded and followed by some little thing . . .'

As my friends and I sit down to lunch—with, yes, a bowl of pasta—we talk of the other elements that help to create this essential air of welcome in a house. It becomes clear that, dreary as it may sound, at least some level of prior housework is necessary. As a person who is quite, shall I say, relaxed about orderliness, piles of stuff on benches or newspapers on coffee tables do not bother me a jot. But the one non-negotiable chore, we decide, is a clean bathroom. Ours sometimes has flowers in it too—but only because the bathroom bench is the only space in the house not covered with stuff, so if someone gives us flowers, that's where they end up. They're also an extravagant surprise when you open the bathroom door.

While on the subject of scrubbing up, there arises the question of what to wear. This provokes some debate among my lunch companions, with the eventual consensus that you should wear whatever the hell you like. But there is agreement that one should, at least, be conscious of how one looks. The bare minimum, we decide, is a clean T-shirt and a quick check in the mirror to eliminate soup from your hair or flour from your eyelashes. All of us, we discovered, tend to make more effort to dress nicely as a guest than we do as a host.

Another idea before opening the door to your guests is a moment's exhalation, relaxation and focus. I love to watch waiters in fine restaurants and how they move, for this very sense of grace.

On the television show *MasterChef*, for example, an experienced maître d' stopped a flurried contestant from rushing to a table with a late dish. *Breathe*, she told her. *Straighten your back. Smile. Now go.* The effect was remarkable.

Some sense of order in the kitchen is an echo of this. I try to have any complex part of the meal cooked well ahead of time. Sometimes, if there have been many guests and many steps involved in the food, I have even gone to the point of chopping herbs and so on in advance and leaving them in a zip-lock bag in the fridge. If that sounds a little Martha-Stewartesque, my defence is that it's all in service to an air of generous harmony for my guests, rather than forcing them to see me rummaging through the crisper on my knees, shrieking that I can't find the fucking parsley as the food cools on the plates. But I'm lucky; my husband is a calm and orderly sous-chef (read: cleaner-upper after me), and now we have the utter decadence of a dishwasher (I will never get over the luxury of it—I want to kiss it every morning), it's not difficult to have a relatively clear space on the kitchen bench. I can say this now we have a new kitchen, but until a couple of years ago I have always cooked in 1940s-era kitchens equipped with a sink and a stove surrounded by a clutter of freestanding cupboards, benches, butcher's blocks and open shelves. Very often when cooking for large numbers of people I have stacked plates on the floor, rested meat on the washing machine and left the dessert in the bedroom. If this is you, fear not: while my own pleasure may have intensified with a new kitchen, that of the guests remains unchanged, and the food is certainly no better.

I am surprised that table-setting turns out to be a matter of hotly contested opinion. I like to set the table before anyone arrives, partly because it's one more job easily got out of the way, and partly because I think a sea of shiny glassware and napkins and cutlery looks welcoming. But I never care about this when I go to someone else's house, and there is a conviviality about having guests set the table that is very pleasant. I always use cloth napkins. I don't know where I developed this habit, because we never used them when I was growing up except on Very Special Occasions. Perhaps I'm a particularly messy eater, but I always feel the lack of a serviette if I don't have one. And cloth is just nicer than paper, though I have many times used paper napkins too.

As I write this I fear it is all perhaps too superficial, or obvious. It certainly seems obvious to me, although when I was very young it didn't. And a friend who cooks dinners for six in people's houses for charity auctions tells me that quite apart from the cooking, many people are incredibly nervous about having guests to dinner at their houses. One wealthy couple, who had spent thousands of dollars on one of these occasions, kept rushing into the kitchen before the guests arrived, asking him in a panic: 'What do we do? We don't know how to do this!'

Once the food is cooked and the guests have arrived, the only thing to focus on is timing. Keeping an eye on wine and water glasses is fairly basic advice, one would think, but people are odd. A couple I once knew were very diligent at topping up their own glasses, then put the wine bottles on a bench behind them, leaving the guests staring for hours into empty glasses.

While being rushed is unpleasant, I think long delays in getting food to the table is a worse crime. I know of a couple of households where the hosts take so long to serve the meal that by the time it arrives you are always either starving, or so stuffed with pre-dinner nibbles that you have no appetite left. Either way, too much has been drunk before eating, always an uncomfortable feeling. Waiting too long for food only makes me anxious and cranky (I am pleased to learn I share this problem with the humorist SJ Perelman, whose letters contain several references to dinners with his friend Dorothy Parker and her husband Alan Campbell. 'They are still eating at two-thirty in the morning; let's not eat right away, shall we, let's have another of these delicious creolin cocktails,' he snarked in 1940. Creolin, apparently, is a general-purpose disinfectant).

Occasionally I detect in the very late serving of food an uncon-scious, rather depressing need to hold people captive, as if once the food has been eaten the dinner guests will all bolt for the hills. But if the first part of lunch is served at four, or dinner at ten, that tends to be exactly what happens, thus reinforcing the desperate need to make it even later the next time. But when I ask my lunch guests about timing, bar one they seem rather more relaxed about it than I am. But the consensus is that there should always be something small to nibble—olives, say—on offer when the guests arrive, and one should begin serving the proper food about an hour after they get there. Definitely within an hour and a half.

If the prompt serving of food is important, equally so, I think, is the release of your guests at their leisure. The generosity of a host extends to allowing people to leave when they want to—yet who hasn't found himself shrieked at when attempting to say goodbye, and poured another glass of undesired wine, and returned, against one's will, to the table? A gracious goodbye, on the other hand, is a gift itself.

CHEAT'S CASSOULET
Serves 8

Dr Pomiane advises: 'Don't blush to offer a cassoulet. Have the courage to serve the most homely dish provided it is perfect of its kind.' This cheat's cassoulet recipe is as far from haute cuisine as it is possible to get—and has been a great favourite among our guests. Do it all well ahead of time and just reheat in the hour before serving, with a simple green salad on the side. If duck is too hard to find, it is just as good with chicken legs.

4 × confit duck legs or fresh duck legs or chicken drumsticks

1 onion, diced

4 cloves garlic, roughly chopped

1 stick celery, diced

1 large carrot, diced

Handful parsley stalks, finely chopped

Olive oil

200 g speck (or pork belly), chopped into chunks

2 × 400 g cans cannellini beans, drained and rinsed

1½ cups chicken stock

1 cup white wine

1 bay leaf

Handful parsley and thyme, chopped

3 pork sausages, cut into big chunks

2 tomatoes, roughly chopped

1–2 cups coarse breadcrumbs

1   Preheat oven to 220°C.

2   Roast duck or chicken pieces for 20–30 minutes or until golden, reserving drippings, and set aside. If using confit duck legs, cut each in half at the thigh joint first.

3   Reduce oven to 180°C.

4   Sauté onion, garlic, celery, carrot and parsley stalks (combination known as a mirepoix) in a little olive oil with a couple of pieces of the speck until soft and a little caramelised. Set aside.

5   In a separate pan, brown the remaining speck pieces until very caramelised, then add to the mirepoix with the beans.

6   Add the stock, wine and herbs and turn off the heat.

7   In the pan you used for the speck, brown the sausage pieces, then add the tomatoes.

8   In a wide, deep casserole dish layer half the bean mixture, followed by half the duck pieces, then add half the sausage and tomato mix.

9   Repeat the layers, then add any remaining stock and wine. There should be enough liquid to just cover the beans—if not, add water.

10 Toss the breadcrumbs through the fat remaining in the duck/chicken pan and spread in a thick layer over the top of the casserole dish.

11 Bake uncovered for about 1 hour or longer, until the breadcrumbs have formed a thick golden crust.

12 Serve at the table in wide, shallow bowls with a green salad on the side.

SPICY FEAST FOR A CROWD

Sometimes when you have more than a few people to dinner, you find yourself needing to account for various dietary issues. This little feast makes vegetarians, gluten-free eaters and omnivores feel loved and it can all be prepared well ahead of time. It will easily feed 10 people. Serve with plain rice or lentils and rice (see page 44) in appropriate quantity.

MILD SALMON CURRY

100 ml rice bran oil

2 teaspoons brown mustard seeds

1 teaspoon fenugreek seeds

8 curry leaves

½ onion, chopped

3 cm knob ginger, finely chopped

3 cloves garlic, finely chopped

Coriander roots and stems, finely chopped

1 teaspoon ground turmeric

2 teaspoons ground coriander

2 teaspoons ground cumin

1 teaspoon paprika

½ teaspoon chilli flakes

Salt

1 fresh birdseye chilli (only because we had a single one on
    our teeeeeny chilli bush—use as many as you like)

½ cup tomato passata

1–2 cups chicken or vegetable stock

1–2 handfuls frozen peas

500 g salmon fillets, pin-boned and cut into large chunks

1 tablespoon natural yoghurt

¼ bunch coriander, chopped

Rice, to serve

Lime wedges, to serve

1   Heat the oil, and when hot toss in the mustard and
    fenugreek seeds and curry leaves. When they start
    to pop and crackle, add the onion, ginger, garlic and
    coriander roots and stems, and cook a few minutes
    until onion is translucent.
2   Add the other spices, salt, fresh chilli, passata and
    stock, and simmer gently, covered, for 20–30 minutes.
3   Toss in the peas and cover to cook for 2–3 minutes.

4 Add the fish pieces, turn the heat off, add the dollop of yoghurt, and leave for a few minutes.

5 When you're quite ready to eat—table set, accompanying rice fluffed and on the table—raise the heat enough to ensure the fish is just cooked, then put the curry in a bowl.

6 Sprinkle with coriander and serve with the lime wedges.

BEETROOT PALAK PANEER

1 medium onion, finely chopped

6 cloves garlic, finely chopped

2 cm knob ginger, finely chopped

2 tablespoons vegetable or olive oil

1 teaspoon cumin seeds

1 teaspoon turmeric

A few curry leaves

1 bunch English spinach, finely chopped

Pinch salt

1 × 400 g can diced tomatoes

1–2 birdseye chillis, roughly chopped

2 medium beetroots, roasted, peeled and cut into chunks

1 small packet paneer (Indian cottage cheese), cubed

Pinch garam masala

1–2 tablespoons dill leaves and stalk, finely chopped

Rice, yoghurt and lemon wedges, to serve

1   Fry onion, garlic and ginger in the oil until soft, then add the spices and curry leaves and fry till aromatic.

2   Add spinach and fry for a few minutes until wilted and coated in the spices, then season liberally with salt.

3   Add tomatoes and chilli and bring to the boil.

4   Add beetroot and simmer gently, covered, for 20–30 minutes for flavours to develop.

5   Add cubed cheese and garam masala and stir to combine.

6   Sprinkle with chopped dill.

7   Serve with rice, yoghurt and lemon wedges on the side.

SPINACH DHAL

This makes a large amount so if it's only for a side dish you may wish to halve the quantities. But as it's even better the next day, I'd suggest you make the lot and you'll have effortlessly delicious lunches for several days.

3 bunches English spinach

2 cups dhal—I used skinned and split moong dahl, but any split lentil will work

1 teaspoon turmeric

1 bay leaf

Vegetable oil

2 teaspoons brown mustard seeds

2 teaspoons cumin seeds

2 or 3 onions, finely chopped

4 cloves garlic, finely chopped

5 cm knob ginger, finely chopped

2 teaspoons salt

1 teaspoon chilli flakes

Green or red chillies, finely chopped, to taste

2 tablespoons shredded coconut

2 ripe tomatoes, chopped

Hot pickle, sweet chutney and chopped coriander, to serve

1   Wash spinach thoroughly, then cut off stems. Keep the stems from one bunch and discard the others. Finely chop the stems and keep separate from the roughly chopped leaves.

2   Combine dhal, turmeric and bay leaf in a pan with water to cover.

3   Stir and bring to a simmer. Cover almost entirely with the lid and leave to simmer gently for up to an hour, or until the lentils are tender.

4   In a separate pan, heat a little oil and fry the mustard and cumin seeds over medium heat until they start to crackle and pop.

5   Add onion, garlic, ginger and spinach stems, and sauté gently until onion is translucent.

6   Put the spinach into the pan, firmly packing it in if necessary, and cover. Cook over gentle heat until the spinach is thoroughly wilted and shrinks right down.

7   When the dhal is cooked, combine the contents of the two pans and mix thoroughly over low heat.

8   Add the remaining ingredients, adjusting seasoning and heat to taste. Continue to cook gently until you achieve the texture you prefer. Add more water if the dhal becomes too thick for your liking.

9   Serve with a dollop of hot pickle or sweet chutney and some chopped coriander.

WHOLE ORANGE CAKE

Serves 10

There are many versions of this recipe, originating with Claudia Roden's classic Middle Eastern orange cake. It's a moist, syrupy slab of a thing—and because there's no flour, it's also suitable for those who can't eat gluten. It takes around an hour to cook, but often longer depending on your oven, and because the oranges take two hours to boil, it's best to make it early in the day.

2 oranges

250 g caster sugar

6 eggs

250 g almond meal

1½ teaspoons baking powder

For dusting cake tin: plain flour (or rice flour for gluten-free cake)

Cream, crushed pistachio nuts, yoghurt or fruit to serve

1 Preheat oven to 150°C.

2 Put oranges into a saucepan and cover with cold water. Cover with a lid, bring to the boil, then boil gently for 2 hours. Drain and allow to cool a little.

3 When oranges are cool enough to handle, cut in quarters, remove any pips and toss the whole segments (including peel) into a food processor.

4 Blend until smooth, then add remaining ingredients and blend until combined thoroughly.

5 Lightly grease a 24 cm springform tin, add a pinch of flour and shake the tin until the base and sides are thoroughly dusted with flour. Tip out any excess flour.

6 Pour the batter into the tin and bake for around 1 hour or longer, until a skewer inserted comes out clean. Cool in the tin before removing the sides of the springform tin.

7 You could smother the top in thick cream and crushed pistachio nuts if you want it to look beautiful, otherwise just slice and serve in shallow bowls with yoghurt or fruit on the side. Or add some excitement with poached quinces or gorgeous stewed rhubarb (see page 147).

A PIE IN THE OVEN:
OVERCOMING FEAR OF PASTRY

What is it about making pastry that inspires such fear—but also such pride—in home cooks?

I have spent most of my adult life shunning the making of pastry as a difficult, messy, stressful task that never yields a good enough result. I don't know why I have been so afraid of it, as I come from a family of good pastry-makers.

My mother excelled at sturdy English-style desserts: puddings, pies and cakes. She could whip up a raspberry tart or an apple pie in minutes, it seemed, and her savoury pastry, too, was crisp, light and flavoursome.

Late in his life even my father became obsessed with pastry—specifically, the traditional hot-water crust pastry necessary for the perfect English pork pie.

Dad's adventures in cooking were never the kind of efficient, no-mess, feed-a-family-of-seven-in-an-hour meals that my mother turned out for decades using little more than a battered aluminium saucepan with no lid and a blunt knife. No, as was customary for

Man Cooks of his generation, Dad's kitchen passions only began to be roused when the children were old enough to wash up after him. His meals were rare and lavish events. Planned over several weeks, they always involved long conversations with the butcher, required the purchase of at least one fancy new cookbook (*The Women's Weekly Chinese Cooking Class*, anyone?) and, preferably, a trip to the big smoke for specialist equipment. My sister Louise recalls driving with him to Canberra—our version of the big city, a good hour or so from home—and being bored rigid while he chatted, seemingly for hours, with the kitchenware shop assistant about his requirements. They came home laden with woks, spatulas, bamboo steamers, cleavers and scrapers. The food he made was spectacular, as was the mess, and I don't recall another Chinese meal after that one.

Our father's pork pie obsession lasted a little longer—possibly because he needed to practise his pastry many times before it reached a satisfactory quality, or possibly because he was a northern English lad and a pork pie must have tasted like home to him. (If you've never eaten a proper cold pork pie, you must. A thick lardy pastry encasing a pink jumble of juicy, luscious lumps of herby pork and bacon, all held together with glassy, cold, salty pork jelly. It's the taste of an Enid Blyton picnic in one bite.)

In my memory the main beneficiaries of these pork pies were my older sister and her best friend, locked away in a distant Catholic boarding school with hordes of teenage girls and a psychotic nun with hyperthyroidism. Every so often a couple of pork pies would be lovingly wrapped in brown paper and dispatched with someone who might be making the big drive to Sydney for delivery en route (if all this sounds a bit horse-and-carty, as if I came of age between the wars instead of the 1980s, you might be getting a bit of a picture of what life was like in Australian country towns back then).

But if that sister received an unfair share of the pork pie bounty, she has redeemed herself many times over. She appears to be the only inheritor of the gene for good pastry—though this could have had as much to do with a gap year in England and the discovery of Delia Smith as with any genetic legacy. Ever since she returned from that trip in her late teens, Bernadette's rough puff pastry has been legendary in our family. Her mince pies each Christmas are precious gifts—irresistible for the density yet crispness of their pastry, and the perfect sweet-tart balance of the fruit.

Only in the last year or so have I become determined to master pastry. Before then, making it always seemed to take forever, and the entire kitchen was covered in flour in the process. My pies ended up torn, patched and lumpy, and very often the pastry didn't cook through on the bottom, leaving me with a good filling but slimy, undercooked dough on the base.

One of the reasons I determined to lose my fear of pastry was the fact that a pie is such a good meal to give someone in a crisis. A pie is a meal in one dish, providing all the necessary protein and vegetable in one hit. Kids love pies, and they satisfy all the criteria of comfort food, loaded with carbohydrate and (one hopes) some good natural fat. In fact, I read recently that it is crucial not to use low-fat ingredients in pastry because their water content makes the dough soggy. A pie is also marvellously versatile, able to be eaten hot or cold for lunch or dinner or a snack, is easy to freeze and to share and can also, if necessary, be loaded with hidden nutrients for picky eaters.

But I think the most important attribute of a homemade pie as first-aid food is the symbolism of it. Even if your pies, like mine, look more as if they were made by a drunk giant wearing mittens than any nimble-fingered pastry chef, there is something comforting about the very *look* of a pie. And a pie is forgiving; a sunken cake just looks depressing, but a lopsided pie, so long as it has a burnished glow, can still project a sort of rustic charm.

I have made many pies for plenty of people using frozen pastry from the supermarket. Some of them looked great, and most tasted just fine, and none of the recipients ever complained about the results. But I knew what my sister's pastry *tasted* like, and my mum's, and my dad's. And given there's almost nobody who'd say no to a homemade chicken pie, or an onion tart or a smoked salmon quiche or a quince and apple tart, I decided I could no longer think of myself as a good home cook if I continued to be intimidated by pastry.

So I asked my sister to give me a rough puff lesson, and I mastered Maggie Beer's famously easy sour cream pastry, and in honour of my father I even learned how to make a serviceable traditional English pork pie with hot-water crust pastry. In doing this I learned that as with all cooking, repetition does indeed promote competence, and from competence comes pleasure. I determined never again to use the cardboard frozen pastry from the supermarket shelf—if I didn't have time to make pastry, I would make something that didn't require it. And I came to understand that a good pie crust is one of the most deeply satisfying things a home cook can make.

In my quest, I learned a few things that might help anyone else who is frightened of pastry. There are references galore for those who love the technical aspect of cooking—all about the structure of gluten and the melting points of various fats, and temperatures and times—but I am not one of those cooks. If you are a proud pastry nerd, the following points will be shamefully inadequate and I advise you to move on. But if you are a mid-level, good home cook like me who just wants to get a grip of your pastry nerves, here are some tips that might help you.

Practice makes pretty good   More than any other thing I've ever made in the kitchen, pastry needs practice. One of the reasons I used to be so disheartened by my occasional attempts was that I only did it once a year, found it stressful and chaotic and the result substandard, and so gave up. But once I decided to really *practise*—giving away many of the results so as not to eat *too* well on butter-laden carbs—I found I began to get a feel for it.

Double the recipe   In my early attempts at pastry I *never* seemed to have enough. This was doubtless because I didn't roll it thinly enough, but the insuffiency meant I tended to stretch and yank the pastry around (a big no-no, I learned later, because it makes the pastry shrink more when cooking), leading to holes and unevenness and leaking filling and a generally grim feeling of failure. But if you make more than enough dough, you always have some left over for the freezer or even just the fridge—it keeps for several days wrapped in cling wrap, ready for rolling in an instant.

Don't rush   Much of my early frustration with pastry, I now realise, arose from impatience. I *hate* waiting, so the idea of chilling things in the fridge for hours on end—and only halfway through a recipe!—used to drive me to distraction, and to damaging shortcuts. But if there's one thing I've accepted about pastry, it is that the fridge is my friend, and the resting and chilling *must not be rushed*. You can't make a pie from scratch in half an hour, because your pastry needs at least an hour and a half's chilling in total. But just a little forethought helps: if you make the dough and refrigerate it before you go shopping for other ingredients, for example, by the time you get home it'll be ready to roll out. The second chilling stage can happen while you're making the filling. And so on. And if you leave it too long because you get held up, it will just need a moment to warm a little on the bench before you roll it.

Ice is nice   With the bizarre (and confusing) exception of hot-water crust pastry, everything to do with all other pastry types must be as icy cold as possible. This includes surfaces, the butter, water, your hands—one friend even keeps her flour in the fridge. There are various pieces of advice about how to keep your hands cold, including keeping an ice-pack handy and holding it every few minutes, as well as working as much as possible only with the fingertips, the coolest part of the hands. It's to do with crispness because of the butter only melting once the pastry is in the oven, but all you need to remember is *colder is better.*

For this reason, best not to make your first attempt on a very hot or humid day—air temperature counts too.

But use a hot oven   Too low a temperature means your pastry will be pale and anaemic-looking. Around 200°C or more is good for a pie, remembering that fan-forced ovens are hotter than those without a fan.

Don't handle it too much   When I was a kid of about ten making scone dough under my mother's distracted supervision, a visiting neighbour remarked on how I was pounding it to death. I was offended by her intrusion, as I think was my mother on my behalf, and she sent the neighbour on her way with a polite coolness I found comforting at the time. But the neighbour was right, and when it comes to pastry even righter—all the rolling, flipping, turning and touching might be pleasurable, but one of the most important rules of pastry, I have learned, is *do not over-handle.*

To lift and move pastry, for example, roll it gently around your rolling pin, then unfurl it over the tin or dish (if your rolling pin is marble, it'll give your biceps a nice workout!).

Give up on pretty   Once I had mastered the texture and taste of a good pie crust, I entered into a brief and foolish fantasy about being One of Those Women who could bake pretty, delicate pies with pastry leaves and perfect rope edges, or little sheaves of wheat decorating the rim. When I badgered my friend Zoe for a little too long about making a perfect pie edging, she finally asked, 'Who are you trying to *impress* with this pie?' She was right. Life's too short for people like me to master pastry wheat sheaves. Rustic is our name.

To blind bake, or not?   For tarts and flans or quiches—anything with no pastry covering—I always blind bake. Which, as you know, means pricking the chilled pastry base, lining with foil or baking paper and then pastry weights or beans/rice and baking for ten or so minutes, removing the weights and then baking for another five minutes or so or until it just begins to colour. This starts crisping the base before a wet filling goes in. For double-crusted pies (ones with a top), you *can* blind bake the base first, but I have found joining the uncooked lid to the half-cooked sides and base a bit of a palaver. Then someone told me to brush the bottom layer before cooking with beaten egg white, chill again for at least ten minutes, then add the filling, join the top by pinching or indenting with a fork, stab a couple of steam holes in the top and bake in the oven. I tested this method alongside a pie where I blind baked the base first, using identical pastry and filling, and found no discernible difference. Both bases were crisp and lovely. The egg white acts as a kind of sealant, it seems, preventing the filling from leaking and softening the base to that hideous sludge you get in processed meat pies.

Balance solids and liquids.   You will get better at this with practice, but try to make sure your filling isn't too wet—you can strain, reduce it or thicken (with a little flour-and-water paste) before filling the pie if it's too runny. A too-wet filling will give you a soggy bottom no matter how blind-baked it is.

MY SISTER BERNIE'S ROUGH PUFF PASTRY

There should be no need to double this recipe but feel free if you want to be safe!

250 g butter, cut into 5 cm chunks (for even richer pastry, replace half the butter with lard)
250 g plain flour
150 ml very cold water
Large pinch salt
Lemon

1 Combine butter, flour and salt in a large bowl, and make a well in the middle into which you pour the icy water and a squeeze of lemon juice.
2 Using a butter knife, 'slash' the mixture together to combine *extremely* roughly, then gather up the mixture and turn it out on to the bench in a big loose, lumpy pile.
3 Push the mixture into a rough rectangle and use a cool rolling pin to roll the dough away from you. Don't roll it back. Lift the pin up and roll it away from you again, gathering in the mixture now and

then to retain the rough rectangular shape. Flour
the rolling pin now and then to stop it sticking.
It's supposed to have giant lumps of butter in it, so
don't panic and do not overwork.

4   Make a quarter turn so one of the longer sides of the
pastry is closest to you. Make two crosswise furrows
using the side of your hand, so your pastry length
now looks like three almost separate plateaus. Then
push the pieces together from the ends, trapping air in
pockets made by the furrows, and roll again.

5   Picture the pastry in thirds, and fold each end third
into the middle to make a fat parcel, then give it
another quarter turn and roll out to its original length.

6   Fold into thirds again, cover with cling film and chill
for at least 20 minutes before rolling into a thickness
of about 3 mm. Line your pie dish/moulds with
pastry, remembering to handle it gently, and chill
again for about an hour before adding the filling.

7   The filling and pastry should be similar temperatures—if your pastry is cold, make sure your filling
has cooled properly. If you blind bake (see above) your
mixture can be hotter.

CHICKEN AND MUSHROOM PIES WITH GREEN PEPPERCORNS

This recipe is also from Bernie and makes about six small pies. If you have chicken mix left over you can freeze it for use another time.

1 quantity rough puff pastry (see page 91), chilled for at least
    20 minutes
1 large or 2 small eggs, whites and yolks beaten separately
2 onions, finely chopped
Olive oil
500 g chicken thigh fillets, cut into 2 cm pieces
2 cups field or Swiss brown mushrooms, chopped
2 tablespoons canned green peppercorns
5 sprigs thyme
300 ml sour cream
Salt and pepper

1   Roll out pastry and line individual pie tins or the holes in a large muffin tin, reserving enough pastry for the pie lids. Roll out pie lids and place on a (cool) floured tray. Brush pie bases with beaten egg white, then refrigerate all for 1 hour.

2   In a pan, sauté onion gently in a little oil until translucent.

3   Raise the heat and add the chicken to onions. Cook over a medium to high heat until just cooked through, then remove both meat and onion from pan and set aside in a large bowl to cool.

4   Return the pan to high heat and add mushrooms. Cook in batches (adding a little more oil if necessary) until well browned, then add to chicken mix.

5   Add peppercorns, thyme, sour cream and seasoning to the chicken and mix all ingredients until well combined, tasting for seasoning as you go. Put mixture in the fridge to cool for at least 10 minutes.

6   Preheat oven to 200°C.

7   Fill pies to the brim with the cooled mixture, and brush pastry rim with egg yolk.

8   Place the chilled pastry lids onto the pies, crimping the edges with a fork and brushing again with egg yolk to seal. Make a couple of small slashes in each lid and brush the whole lid lightly with egg yolk.

9   Bake in a preheated hot oven (around 200°C) for about 25 minutes or until pies are golden brown. If you fear the edges will burn, make an aluminium foil ring to cover the edges for the first half of the cooking.

10 Cool pies in their tins on a rack for 10 minutes or until cool enough to handle, then turn pies out. Serve with a green salad.

Silverbeet/Swiss chard tart

Serves 6

1 quantity rough puff pastry (see page 91), chilled for at least
   20 minutes
1 onion, finely chopped
½ bunch silverbeet (Swiss chard), leaves and stems separated and chopped
2 tablespoons chopped bacon, optional
1 cup natural yoghurt
6 eggs, beaten
Salt and pepper

1   Roll out pastry and line a 23 cm flan or quiche tin,
    chill and blind bake as described on page 91, and set
    aside. Lower oven to 180°C.

2   In a pan, sauté onion, chopped silverbeet stems (and
    bacon if using) until soft.

3   Add chopped leaves and stir until lightly wilted.

4   In a large bowl, combine yoghurt, beaten eggs and
    silverbeet mixture, and mix well. Season.

5   Turn mixture into warm pastry case and return
    to oven.

6   Bake for about 30 minutes or until golden.

BEEF AND RED WINE PIES
Serves 6

This recipe is adapted from Maggie Beer's Coorong Angus beef pie with red wine, fennel and green olives.

1 quantity rough puff pastry (see page 91) (half-lard, half-
   butter is best for this pie)
1 egg, lightly beaten
1 kg beef cheeks, trimmed
Olive oil
2 sticks celery, finely chopped
4 cloves garlic
1 carrot, finely chopped
1 medium fennel bulb, finely chopped
4 golden shallots, finely chopped
400 ml red wine
5 sprigs thyme
3 cloves
zest of ½ large orange
2 cups chicken stock

1   Roll out pastry and line 6 individual pie tins or as
    many spaces in a large muffin tin, reserving enough
    pastry for the pie lids. Roll out pie lids and place on

a (cool) floured tray. Brush pie bases with beaten egg, refrigerate all for 1 hour.

2   In a cast-iron casserole or heavy-bottomed frypan, brown meat thoroughly in olive oil over high heat. Remove meat and set aside.

3   Reduce the heat to low and fry celery, garlic, carrot, fennel and shallots in the same pan until soft, adding a little more oil if necessary.

4   Add red wine a little at a time, and simmer until well reduced.

5   Return meat to pan with thyme, cloves and orange zest.

6   Add stock and stir to combine.

7   Cook in moderate oven for 2 hours or until the meat is tender enough to part with a spoon. Check every half hour or so, adding a little water if the meat appears to be drying out.

8   Use a spoon to break the meat apart into an even mix, remove from casserole and cool completely.

9   Spoon cooled meat into cases, add pastry lids, folding over and sealing with a fork or by pinching. Brush tops with beaten egg and return to fridge for 20 minutes.

10   Preheat the oven to 220°C. Bake pies for 20–30 minutes or until rich golden, putting a tray underneath to catch any dripping fat.

11 Remove pies from oven and allow to sit in the tins for 10 minutes or so before removing—check bases are coloured enough. If not, return to oven, covering tops loosely with foil if necessary to prevent burning.

REGAINING YOUR KITCHEN MOJO: THE CHICKEN-STOCK METHOD

R ecently, a friend remarked rather sadly that it seemed she never cooked anymore.

She works hard at a stressful job, and her partner is a good cook who is happy to take on the bulk of the cooking. But these weren't the only reasons she had virtually abandoned the pots and pans. The more troubling thing, she said, was that despite having been an excellent cook at various times of her life, it seemed now she had simply lost the zest for it, and didn't know how to get it back.

Even the most dedicated cook knows how this feels, I think. There have been days, even weeks sometimes, when I have searched my mind for an idea for dinner and come up with only two possibilities: grilled chicken thighs or pesto—both of which I have already eaten that week. In this malaise, it's not that you don't want to cook other things—more that you simply can't imagine what other things there might *be* to cook. The recipe books on your shelves are like holiday brochures: full of beautiful places you might like to visit one day, but which are simply too distant, too exotic, too out of reach for now.

I find this a very melancholy syndrome, and a cumulative one; the lack of activity and achievement soon accelerates, pushing me quickly into deeper blues. In its early stages, it is characterised by a light fog of gloom, which turns to overwhelming fatigue whenever one catches sight of the oven. It can last for years, and the same cure doesn't work for everyone.

Fortunately there are a few remedies that might, slowly but surely, restore the sufferer's confidence and enthusiasm for cookery.

In the same week my friend told me of her culinary ennui, I found myself in the throes of a syndrome at the opposite end of the spectrum—an episode of insomnia which saw me lying awake at 3 am, rigid with excitement about a bag of chicken bones in the fridge.

This was partly inspired by one of my brothers-in-law marvelling over why people paid good money for cartons of stock full of salt and preservatives when chicken stock was so simple to make. I had to confess to being one of those ninnies; I had not made stock for months, and often used carton stock (I still think, by the way, that this is pretty far down the list of culinary sins). But of course he was correct about it being so easy to make, and cheap. I realised that even the organic and free-range meat suppliers I support might willingly sell me some bones. And so it was that a bag of four beautiful, fresh, meaty, free-range chicken carcases landed on my doorstep—for the princely sum of five dollars.

As I flung the little pink carcases into two big stock pots along with the other bits and bobs, it occurred to me that perhaps making a pot of chicken stock might be a step towards regaining one's vanished culinary mojo.

There are several reasons behind this theory. First, making stock involves no imperative to actually complete a whole meal, and there could be little less demanding work than halving a carrot, an onion, a celery stick and a tomato and tossing them into a pot with a couple of handfuls of herbs (bay leaf, thyme, parsley, whatever), the chicken bones and some water. Second, the sensory delight of this task is immense. For one thing, there's the smell—our front door was open to the street when I made mine, and more than once passers-by stopped and peered into the house, calling that it smelled delicious. Then there's the visual appeal—the glistening baubles of fat separating and rejoining, the gentle steam, the gradual transformation of your wan bunch of ingredients into a potful of gold.

But most importantly, I think making stock provides an instant and very rewarding culinary pride. Despite its utter simplicity, homemade stock makes one feel like a real cook. It's partly to do with the busy productivity of the water toiling and simmering away, while all you really need do is read detective novels on the couch with a cup of coffee or a glass of wine. It's also to do with the virtue involved in making wholesome good use of otherwise wasted vegetable crisper odds and ends—those tough bits of leek, nubs of carrots, limp herbs and otherwise useless parsley stalks, mushroom trimmings and overripe tomatoes. And partly, of course, it's the incredible usefulness of the result: a splash or a litre of homemade stock can enrich anything from a pasta sauce to a tagine to poaching broth to bouillabaisse to minestrone.

The other advantage of the chicken-stock method of mojo revival is that you can enter into the kitchen spirit without the need for performance. There's no tricky timing to worry about, no dinner-party stress, no anxiety about the possibility of a raised eyebrow from your partner, housemate or cat—for as there is no right recipe, there's no right result (a good rich vegetable stock can be almost as satisfying to make, I think, and the result is most definitely as useful).

But making stock is not the only way to fan the dying embers of cookery enthusiasm. Here are some other methods.

Have a well stocked pantry and freezer That way, when inspiration strikes there's no dreary going to the shops involved. Let's face it, car parks and supermarkets can drain the life force out of the most committed cooks, so removing that giant obstacle is sometimes all that's needed (I have been asked so many times for a list of pantry essentials that I have included one on pages 127–129, but every cook has her own—I always ask my friends what theirs are; the answers can be surprising).

Start small Adding a little interest to otherwise simple dishes can help rebuild confidence. For me, even sparking up a green salad with a few toasted nuts, a sprinkling of Puy lentils or a lump or two of goat's cheese is satisfying enough to nudge me into trying something new for the next dish.

Immersion and inspiration   I find a trip to a growers' or farmers' market, or even just a really good grocer, can be enough to get the cook's blood flowing in the veins again. All that freshness and bounty, and the fact that markets are stuffed full of other people who are excited about food, is contagious.

Use good equipment   No kitchen needs lots of gadgets, and the cooking gear need not be expensive, but decent saucepans, at least one sharp chef's knife and a sturdy food processor can make otherwise tiresome chores easy and pleasurable.

Watch a little Maggie Beer or Jamie Oliver   Both cooks have an exuberant belief in the joys of uncomplicated cooking and an egalitarian insistence that anyone can cook good food. Whenever I see them speak or read their recipes I feel the urge to cook.

But maybe all this insistence on getting into the kitchen could be trying too hard. My friend Zoe, one of the most adventurous cooks I know, says: 'If you draw creative satisfaction from cookery, you need to understand that as with all creative processes there will be ebbs and flows. It has happened to me many times. I've learned to sit it out.'

CHICKEN STOCK

Vegetables in a stock can vary according to what you have in the fridge—I have often added fennel stalks, knobs of ginger, leek, chilli and other bits and pieces to a stock. These are just the basics. If you are going to freeze the stock (it only lasts two to three days in the fridge, but months if frozen), don't forget to use a few small containers for when you just need a little bit. Yoghurt or ice-cream tubs are good as you can easily remove partially thawed stock and fling it in a soup, for example, but bottles are fine if you don't mind having to thoroughly thaw the stock before using.

Raw or cooked chicken bones (raw are best—fresh chicken wings are excellent for stock—but the leftover bones from a roast chicken are good too)
1 onion, halved
1 carrot, halved
1 tomato, halved
1 large stick celery, broken into pieces
A few parsley stalks
Some thyme sprigs
2 bay leaves
6 peppercorns
Salt

1   Cover the chicken bones generously with water and bring to a boil, then reduce to a simmer.

2   When the stock has been simmering for around 10 minutes, skim as much of the discoloured foam from the surface as you can.

3   Add remaining ingredients and simmer on the lowest heat for several hours.

4   Check seasoning. If you wish, reduce the stock to concentrate its flavour; otherwise strain and allow to cool.

5   When cold, remove fat from the surface and pour into containers for freezing.

ROASTED VEGETABLE STOCK

My vegetable stock used to be so wan as to be almost flavourless, until I began roasting the vegetables first. Then I took a leaf from Australian-British cook Skye Gyngell's book and added a spoonful each of tamari sauce and maple syrup right at the end. The result is a rich dark stock with loads of flavour.

Assorted vegetables—whatever you have in the fridge. My last batch included carrots, shallots, pumpkin with the skin on, red onion, garlic, celery, a bunch of spinach stems and an overripe tomato

Olive oil

2 bay leaves

5 peppercorns

Handful of herbs—thyme, tarragon, rosemary, parsley stalks

1 tablespoon tamari sauce (or regular soy sauce)

1 tablespoon maple syrup

Salt

1   Preheat oven to 200°C.

2   Toss vegetables into a roasting pan, coat well with olive oil and roast for at least 30 minutes.

3   Once the vegetables have begun to caramelise well, remove from oven and turn into a large pot of water.

4   Add the herbs and peppercorns and bring to a boil.

5   Simmer for at least 2 hours or more, reducing by a third, topping up with water and reducing again, then straining it.

6   Add the tamari and maple syrup and season well.

HOW TO ROAST A CHICKEN

In seventeenth-century France, Good King Henry IV promised his subjects that so long as he reigned, 'I will make sure that there is no working man in my kingdom who does not have the means to have a chicken in the pot every Sunday.' I like this idea of a chicken dinner as a symbol of genteel comfort and social order. No matter how hardscrabble and poor the working week may have been, King Henry seems to be saying, when Sunday and a chicken dinner comes, all will be right with the world.

Despite the Englishness of our parents, in our house growing up there was no tradition of the Sunday roast. Roast chicken, in fact, was a very special meal, eaten on birthdays and at Christmas. I suppose this was mainly an economical decision, for four decades ago chicken was not cheap unless you reared your own. Nor was chicken farming the depressingly vast enterprise it is today; in the 1960s and 70s chickens had better lives and took far longer to grow to eating size. As well, in our small country town, fast-food chicken chains—even independent barbecue chicken shops, if I recall rightly—did not spring up until we were well out of high school.

But I like to think it wasn't only cost that made roast chicken an exceptional, festive treat in our house—perhaps our mother also liked the idea of keeping a particular meal separate for special occasions, and starting her own tradition of a celebration family meal. Whatever her motive, it worked—although we eat it quite often today, I think all my siblings and their kids still think of roast chicken as the ultimate combination of luxury and comfort.

And it's not just our family. I think I have a higher strike rate in dinner acceptances if my guests see the words 'roast chicken' in the email subject line. For a time some years ago, a group of our friends would gather for a regular dinner of roast chook that became known as 'the family roast', with all the easeful pleasure conjured by the image (if not, for some families, the reality!).

But I have recently come to understand that many people don't see roasting a chicken as easy or pleasurable at all—that, in fact, many otherwise perfectly competent home cooks see it as intimidating and stressful. There appear to be several aspects that frighten people.

First, there's the perceived issue of tricky timing—a misconception that all the vegetables and meat must reach a state of perfect readiness at exactly the same time for the meal to succeed. In fact, once a chicken (or almost any meat) is roasted, it is only improved by resting under a loose covering of foil on top of the stove or another warm place for quite long periods of time while you wait for other things to cook. I take the same laissez faire approach to roasting vegetables, pulling them out of the oven at various times if I think they are cooking too fast for the meat or other vegetables to catch up, and only putting them back in when I feel like it.

Second is the related issue of needless panic about bringing food to the table piping hot. This is perhaps a hangover from our childhoods—the phrase *eat it while it's hot!* had an almost medical urgency about it in our house. But think about dining out in restaurants: most of the time, if restaurant food arrives at your table so hot it burns your mouth, it's a signal it's come straight from a microwave. Not a good sign. Once this was explained to me, I completely relaxed about the serving temperature of food at home. I do, though, maintain an obsession of my mother's: I almost always serve food on hot plates (I heat them—those in possession of posh crockery may weep—in the microwave for a couple of minutes).

Third, there seems—particularly with chicken—to be a widespread and quite irrational anxiety about being poisoned by undercooked meat. Although the fear of pink flesh has largely disappeared with red meat, we still seem to have a terror of it in chicken. Of course a chicken should be properly cooked, but meat near the bone will be darker and often pinker than breast meat. A chicken is cooked if the juices run clear when a skewer is inserted into the thigh meat, but the best way to check for doneness is with a meat thermometer. Most sources say chicken meat is cooked at about 73–76°Celsius. But the heat in the meat will continue to cook it once removed from the oven, so taking it out at a few degrees earlier—even at 68°C, according to Maggie Beer—will help prevent overcooking.

The fourth factor, I think, could simply be exhaustion at the idea of preparing a Roast Dinner. This comes from trying to do too much: the famous 'trimmings' of a roast dinner, which are almost always quite unnecessary. Two or three accompanying vegetables are plenty, for example, and in the contemporary roast dinner, stuffing and gravy are entirely optional accompaniments. I never make 'proper' gravy—usually I simply deglaze the pan with a bit of wine, sometimes but not always adding some stock, and raise the heat for five or ten minutes until a loose, light sauce of pan juices results. But if the chicken is succulent, rather than dry, no sauce is necessary at all. Nor should the whole thing take many hours to prepare; once in the oven, a roast chicken need not take longer than an hour and a half to reach the table.

The final problem—I think it's actually the most difficult part of the whole enterprise—is the *carving* of the chicken. The bird may look perfectly delicious once out of the oven and rested, but in my house a carving approach more akin to murderous dismemberment than elegant portioning has reduced the aesthetic appeal of many a roasted bird and, worse, raised the stress level just when one should be relaxing and sitting down to eat. But a few rounds of internet how-to videos, a little research and some practice has largely fixed this for me. If you too have carving problems, the tips below might help.

Part of the pleasure of roasting a chicken is the warmth of the room and the delicious smell spreading through the house as it cooks. When my friend Lu's father was ill, she and her brother took many prepared meals to their parents' house and left them in the fridge. But while the nourishment was welcome, after a little while the parents grew dispirited by the endless reheating of cooked food, so one evening Lu and her husband drove to the house with a fresh uncooked chicken and a roasting tray full of prepared vegetables in oil, to be joined there by her brother for a family meal. The gift was threefold: her parents received not only an excellent meal without the work, but could relish the chickeny aromas wafting through the house as it cooked—and, perhaps most importantly, it allowed them to offer, not just receive, hospitality once more.

It's my opinion that every cook should have a well-made roast chicken in his or her repertoire. Able to carry endless variations of flavour and style, it is perhaps the most versatile and elegant comfort food of all.

HOW TO ROAST A CHICKEN

Heat the oven to 220°C. Remove the chicken from its packaging, rinse and pat dry inside and out. Rub the chicken all over with a little soft butter and salt or, as Stephanie Alexander suggests, scrub it all over with a lemon half and then some olive oil. Into the cavity put one or two lemon halves, a couple of squashed garlic cloves, a sprig or two of rosemary, thyme and/or other herbs. Put the chicken into the dish, perhaps sitting atop a few chunks of onion or shallot to stop it sticking, with optional other vegetables surrounding the bird. Some cooks recommend starting with the chicken breast side down for the first 20 minutes before reducing the heat to 180°C, returning the chicken to breast side up and continuing to cook. Roast for a further 40 minutes or until the juices run clear from the thigh (or a meat thermometer measures 73°C). When ready, remove the chicken from the pan and rest in a warm shallow dish, breast-side down again, for 20 minutes to half an hour before carving.

ACCOMPANIMENTS

While the chicken is resting, pour off some of the clear fat from the roasting pan, then set the pan over one or two burners on a medium heat and toss in a glassful of white wine, scraping and stirring vigorously to loosen the caramelised morsels of fat and skin and any vegetable bits. Add a cup or two of chicken stock, or more wine or water, and boil vigorously, stirring, until the sauce has reduced a little. You are after a pan full of luscious juices, not a thick gravy. Add any juices that have collected in the chicken's resting plate to the sauce before carving the bird and arranging it on a large platter. Pour the juices over the meat (reserving any excess to serve at the table in a jug) and take the platter to the table. If even this sounds like too much effort, simply carve the chicken and serve without a dressing—or with a bowl of aioli or mayonnaise, or tzatziki or a herby yoghurt dressing.

For a roast chicken involving a little more effort, try spreading a herbed butter beneath the skin of the bird before you cook it. Mix around 100 g softened butter with finely chopped garlic, thyme, tarragon or rosemary (or all three). With the legs pointing towards you, use your fingers to gently open up the pocket of skin at the breast, slowly easing a space between the flesh and the skin without tearing it. Into this pocket on each side of the breastbone, spoon a lump of the butter and then, with your fingers outside the skin once more and holding the pocket closed, smooth the butter beneath the skin over the breast and down towards the legs. Repeat on the other side, and then rub any remaining butter over the outside of the whole bird. Maggie Beer sometimes adds finely chopped preserved lemon to her butter, while Neil Perry adds spices, saffron and lemon zest.

Good vegetables to accompany roast chicken include the classics of potatoes, carrots, parsnip and pumpkin, of course, but I love also the aniseed sharpness of quartered fennel and the sweet bursting squishiness of zucchini (add the latter, cut into thirds, only about thirty minutes or so before the cooking is finished). Recently I fed two starving young university students on chicken roasted with fennel through which I had tossed a few rounds of chorizo sausage before cooking. Never has such a simple meal been so highly praised.

CARVING

Don't carve at the table It's way too much pressure, and you can't wrangle the bird efficiently without elbow room and lots of space. Carve it near the oven, keeping the meat warm in a pan on the stove top as you go, then serve from a platter in the centre of the table when it's all done. A much more restful experience for everyone.

Ensure your knife is very sharp Use a good large cook's or boning knife, and sharpen it as much as possible before you begin. A blunt knife and slippery chicken skin is a dangerous combination, whereas a sharp one will find instant purchase.

Use your (clean, naturellement!) hands The effective carving of a chicken needs a little anatomical understanding, and this can be found much more easily by following the bones and joints with your fingers. For example, if you pull the leg quite widely out from the body of the bird, it will either simply pull away entirely, or the end of the leg joint, and where to cut it, will be clearly revealed. The same happens when you want to cut the drumstick away from the thigh—use your fingers to gently bend the leg and you'll see the joint, and the best place to cut. Make sure you have a clean tea towel for frequent wiping of oil from your fingers so the knife won't slip in your hands. I recommend watching a couple of internet videos to see how to section the chicken—the ones by Kay Chun of *Gourmet* and Marc Bauer of the French Culinary Institute are particularly good (for those who prefer not to get physical with their food, Bauer doesn't use his hands).

Work on an appropriate surface   Move the chicken from the pan onto a cutting board to carve it, ensuring that its juices won't run all over the bench. Stopping mid-carve to mop up juices with one hand while pinioning a chicken to the board with a knife in the other, all the while bending awkwardly to avoid chicken drippings on your jeans, is way too chaotic and dangerous. I have a carving board with a tilted surface and a liquid-collecting area, and I've seen other fancy boards that drain meat juices into a separate little cruet. But if you don't have one of these, you need only position the board on a wet cloth or some paper towel to catch any drips, to keep your focus on the carving rather than the cleaning.

Cut breast meat across the grain, not with   The classic way of slicing breast meat longways, as our fathers used to do at the table (why *was* carving always left to men who had no other discernible skill with food?), tears the meat and allows it to dry out quickly. Better to remove the breast from the bone in one piece, simultaneously cutting both downwards and nudging the meat away from the breastbone. Taking the wing off together with the breast also makes it easier to see the joint where the wing can be removed. Once you have removed the whole breast, slice it crossways, on a slight angle, into two or more little chunks. It looks neater, and there's less surface area from which to lose the juice.

BRINING

Brining of poultry and other meats is very popular in the US, but is catching on in Australia too, as a way to ensure meat remains as succulent as possible. Brining also allows another very subtle layer of flavouring with herbs, spices and citrus. (For instructions on how to brine a chicken see page 11).

FRUIT WITH ME DINNER

In the weeks after the funeral, when the girls are gone, the thing Ralph can't get used to is opening up the fridge. It's well stocked by church friends but it's all strangers' food—and, worse, increasingly the dishes arrive named after other countries. An unspoken competition has begun between members of the Ladies' Auxiliary, who compete with recipes cut from newspapers and magazines. Confronted by Pork Hawaiian, Ralph decides he does not like having his main course doubling as dessert.

The Reverend Ralph Cage, in Vicki Hastrich's sublime novel *The Great Arch,* could be speaking for more than one generation of men with his aversion to the melding of sweet and savoury in a main course. This scene is set in 1962, when Pork Hawaiian was all the rage. Three decades later, a family friend of mine was presented with the classic appetiser of a slice of rockmelon wrapped in a salty, satiny ribbon of San Daniele prosciutto. Even the fact of its being prepared for him by two glamorous young women visiting from Italy wasn't enough to impress Pete, who looked down at his plate with open distaste, arms folded. 'Nah thanks, mate,' he said. 'I don't eat fruit with me dinner.'

When I was young I was in league with Ralph and Pete on this issue. Reared on the kind of food where dinner was dinner and pudding came after, to my country girl's palate the mixing of sweet and savoury was—unnatural. But looking back, I think we had good reason to be suspicious, because Australian cookery of the 1970s and 80s was awash with quite revolting sweet-and-meat concoctions. Consider this recipe for that staple of the progressive dinner party, apricot chicken:

Take 8 chicken legs, 1 packet dried French onion soup mix, 1 tin apricot nectar, 1 tin apricot halves. Mix soup and the apricot nectar and pour over the chicken pieces. Bake 40 minutes, add drained apricot halves and serve.

The result of this kind of recipe, if memory serves correctly, was a mess of lurid orange gloop so sweet it made your teeth hurt, with a faint aftertaste of preservative 2345.

And what about poor Reverend Ralph's Pork Hawaiian? Cubed pork, red and yellow capsicum, pineapple juice, pineapple chunks. You really can't blame him for his culinary xenophobia after that confection. I do love Hastrich's acute observation here about the dishes being named so bluntly after countries—in an exercise book of jotted recipes and clippings begun in 1959 lent to me by a friend there is a carefully handwritten recipe for Italian Rice with Roman Cheese. This was later to become more familiar to us as 'risotto'.

I think my parents, being of good English stock, were as suspicious as Ralph about combining meat and fruit. Sultanas in rice? Apricots and chicken? Hawaiian steak? Sweet and sour pork? No thank you—all a little too exotic, too modern, for our traditional tastes. But of course we were wrong. If we had stopped to think about it we would have seen just how English, and how age-old, were various combinations of fruit and meat, sugar and salt: cranberry sauce with turkey, chutney on a ham sandwich, mint sauce with lamb and apple sauce with pork—even the delectable devil on horseback and the classic duck à l'orange—to name just a few obvious ones.

Mixing fruit and meat or sweet and savoury was common, apparently, right back to medieval and Renaissance times, not just in Britain but everywhere in Europe. Apples, quinces, figs, oranges, peaches, pears, raisins and pomegranates abound in savoury Spanish recipes of the Middle Ages, and the French, English and Italians threw plums, figs, dates, prunes and raisins into meat dishes. The original Christmas mince pie and the forerunner of plum pudding (a plum 'porridge') were mixtures of meat and fruit, the sugar in the latter helping not only to preserve the meat, but possibly to mask its taste when a little too aged for eating alone.

I'm not quite sure what made me overcome my own hostility towards mixing meat and fruit—perhaps the simple fact of growing up, along with moving to a city abundant in cheap 'ethnic' restaurants where I began to discover that all the cuisines I loved were big on sweet and savoury. Not the gluggy, syrupy version of sweet-and-sour everything that has ruined many a country kid's attitude towards Chinese food (the MSG-glossy blanket of sugar and canned pineapple over fried pork blobs in the typical country RSL Club restaurant of the 70s and 80s—ugh), but cuisines where the *balance* of sweet and salt and sour and spice was paramount. Enter Indian pilafs and Thai stir-fries along with Moroccan tagines or Italy's figs and prosciutto.

More recently, Australia's love affair with Middle Eastern food has led me to use lots more dried fruit in my own cooking, as has Maggie Beer, with her predilection for tossing citrus peel or quinces or pears or verjuice into so many savoury dishes. And I've found that in cooking for friends, the main courses they most often swoon over are those dishes that include a little bit of fruit—currants, raisins, prunes or citrus peel. Crucially, the sweetness in these recipes is always balanced by the sharpness of lemon, the heat of chilli or ginger, the complexity of other spice mixes and, most importantly, adequate seasoning with *salt*. To my mind it's this that has consigned apricot chicken to the retro joke book, yet allows the devil on horseback its classic status: the lack of saltiness in the former and abundance in the latter.

Following are some of my favourite fruit-and-savoury combinations. Even the Reverend Ralph Cage might approve.

LAMB TAGINE WITH DATES AND RAISINS

Serves 8

1–2 boned lamb shoulders (about 2 kg), cut into large
    chunks

Olive oil

2 onions, finely chopped

4 cloves garlic, finely chopped

7 cm knob ginger, very finely julienned

1 bunch coriander stems and roots, finely chopped

1 teaspoon turmeric

2 teaspoons ground cumin

2 teaspoons cinnamon

2 teaspoons ground coriander

1 teaspoon paprika

1 large pinch saffron

2 teaspoons salt

2 fresh birdseye chillis, split lengthwise

2 cups chicken stock

Juice of 1 lemon

10 large green olives

6 dates, pitted and halved

2 tablespoons raisins

2 tablespoons maple syrup

Salt and pepper

1 bunch coriander leaves, chopped

2 tablespoons slivered almonds

Couscous, to serve

1   In a heavy-based pan brown meat in olive oil over high heat, then remove meat and set aside.

2   Lower heat and fry onion, garlic, ginger, and coriander roots and stems until soft.

3   Add spices, salt and chillies and cook over moderate heat until fragrant.

4   Return meat to pan and add chicken stock.

5   Bring to a low simmer, cover and cook for 1–2 hours or until meat is very tender. Top up liquid with water if it seems to be drying out at any time.

6   About 20 minutes before the end, add the lemon juice, olives, dates and raisins.

7   Reduce liquid until the sauce is slightly thickened.

8   Taste, then add maple syrup a little at a time, making sure the tagine is not too sweet. Balance out the sweetness by seasoning well with salt and pepper.

9   Garnish the tagine with chopped coriander and sprinkle the slivered almonds over, and serve from the pot at the table. Serve with fluffy couscous (see page 264).

CHICKEN MARBELLA

Serves 6–8

I believe the original recipe was from The Silver Palate Cookbook, *first published in the 1980s, but variations abound. This one is adapted from one given to me by a colleague many years ago. Its finest moment came when, during a camping drive across the Nullarbor Plain a decade ago, I crashed our car and stranded us in the pouring rain on a dirt road in the middle of nowhere. Luckily, this had been marinating in the chiller; we might have been stranded in the South Australian desert, out of phone range and with four flat tyres, but we had good food and good wine. This dish became known that night as Chicken Maralinga, but don't let that put you off—it's delectable.*

1.5 kg chicken thighs and drumsticks

1 head garlic, peeled and crushed

¼ cup dried oregano

½ cup red wine vinegar

½ cup olive oil

1 cup pitted prunes

1 cup pitted green olives

½ cup capers, with a little of their brine

6 fresh bay leaves

1 chorizo sausage, sliced into 3 mm rounds

¼ cup brown sugar

½ cup white wine

Salt and pepper

Handful parsley, finely chopped

Handful coriander, finely chopped

1   Combine chicken, garlic, oregano, vinegar, olive oil, prunes, olives, capers and bay leaves in a large bowl and mix thoroughly to combine. Cover with plastic wrap and marinate overnight in the fridge.

2   Preheat oven to 180°C.

3   Fry chorizo slices in a non-stick pan over medium-high heat until well browned, then set aside.

4   In the same pan, brown the chicken pieces, then arrange them in a single layer in one or two roasting trays, spooning the marinated residue over the meat.

5   Sprinkle brown sugar over the pieces, scatter the chorizo slices into the tray/s and pour white wine around them.

6   Bake for 20–30 minutes or until chicken is cooked. Season to taste and garnish with chopped herbs.

7   Optional: If you have a lot of marinade remaining, you can reduce it to a sauce by simmering on the stove top while you rest the meat under a loose covering of foil for about 10 minutes. Pour the sauce over the chicken before serving from a wide shallow dish at the table.

SARDINES, SICILIAN STYLE

Serves 4–6

Olive oil

1 cup breadcrumbs

½ cup currants, plumped for a few minutes in verjuice or
water

½ cup pine nuts, toasted

½ bunch parsley, finely chopped

1 tablespoon thyme leaves, picked

Salt and pepper

12 large fresh sardines, cleaned and butterflied but not
completely split

1   Preheat oven to 180°C.

2   Heat a few glugs of oil over medium-high heat.
When oil is hot, add breadcrumbs and cook, stirring,
until lightly toasted. Remove from heat and set aside
in a bowl.

3   Add currants, pine nuts, parsley and thyme to breadcrumbs. Season with salt and pepper.

4   Line an oven tray with baking paper and lay sardines
on it.

5   Fill the cavity of each sardine with breadcrumb
mixture and fold it closed. Sprinkle remaining breadcrumbs over sardines and drizzle generously with oil.

6   Bake until sardines are cooked through and hot, about 20 minutes. Remove from oven and serve from a large platter immediately.

FIGS AND PROSCIUTTO, FIGS AND ROCKMELON

Ripe fresh figs
Slices of ripe rockmelon
Prosciutto—the best you can find—very thinly sliced

1   Cut figs into halves or quarters, winding a strip of prosciutto around each one. Do the same with rockmelon slices. Add either to a cheese platter or serve on their own as the simplest appetiser in the world.

SEE ALSO
Devils on horseback (see page 231)
Jane's citrus couscous (see page 264)
Quinoa salad (see page 265)

ESSENTIAL INGREDIENTS

🍎

I have always wanted a larder, despite never actually thinking about what it might be, exactly. I suppose it is 'lard' which makes it sounds so much more abundant and plentiful than 'pantry', which makes me think of 'paltry'. When I check the definitions, of course, it's blindingly obvious: a larder was a cool room for storing meat, and a pantry (from the French *pain*) for storing bread and other foods associated with it. Rather less obviously, some references say a buttery was used to store not dairy goods but alcohol (for the 'butts' of barrels stored there). Now this is clear to me, I would still like a larder as well as a pantry and certainly a buttery (a scullery, with its maid, would also be welcome). Living in a small inner-city house rather than a country mansion, however, I shall have to make do with the pantry cupboard and refrigerator.

You can tell a lot about a person from her pantry, I've found. As I love a little pry into the pantry cupboards and freezers of other cooks—every good cook has some surprise staples—and friends have sometimes asked me what I regard as the essential ingredients of cooking, here's my list. Apart from the obvious boring things like canned tomatoes, pasta and rice, these are the essentials I am never without.

IN THE PANTRY

Currants, dried cranberries   My friend Caro introduced me to dried cranberries and now I find them indispensable, plumped with vinegar, in couscous and quinoa salads because of their ruby-red beauty and sweetness. Currants have a darker, more complex flavour and I put them in anything vaguely Middle Eastern. Plumped with vinegar or water they are also lovely sprinkled through a green salad, especially one with strong-tasting leaves. Vinegar-soaked and fried with chopped red onion, celery and breadcrumbs, they make whiting or sardine fillets into sweet Sicilian heaven.

Stock—cartons or cubes   Yes, it's too salty; yes, it's got preservatives in it; yes, making your own is far, far superior. But sometimes you just don't, and in that case packaged stock is completely fine. One or two little cartons are always in our pantry.

Spices   Turmeric, cumin seeds (toasting them for a few seconds and then grinding gives an amazing flavour, so much more powerful than the powdered cumin, though I use both), coriander seeds and ground, chilli flakes, cinnamon sticks and dried chipotle chillies.

Lentils, dried   As detailed elsewhere, the French-style blue lentil is a thing of beauty. Braise them for a dish in their own right (see page 41), use in salads or simply turn a tablespoonful of olive oil through a cup of cooked lentils and toss into a pan of roasted vegetables. For dhal I mostly use the satiny, creamy little moong dhal lentils, although they can be hard to find. Yellow split peas are almost as good.

Quinoa   I've become obsessed with the springy texture and nutty flavour of quinoa, mostly using it in place of couscous. It is a little pricey and can be hard to find, although even our supermarket now sells three varieties in the 'natural foods' section. The red, black and white cook at slightly different rates—but I mix them and cook together because I like the variable texture.

Capers and anchovies   Salt bombs. Anchovies soaked in orange juice for five minutes and chopped are incredible sprinkled through a green salad, and the little opened flowers of fried capers are beautiful not only to eat but to look at.

Chickpeas, cannellini beans and lentils, canned   For salads and boofing up soups when you are out of time or can't be bothered soaking the dried ones. Rinse and rinse before using. Simply substituting chickpeas for meat protein in recipes works well more often than you'd think—especially in tagines, curries and any casserole with a kick of spice.

Red wine, balsamic and raspberry vinegar   My friend Eileen converted me to raspberry vinegar—it is luscious in dressings on strong, peppery leaves like spinach, rocket and sorrel. Eileen has a secret supplier of pure—not flavoured—raspberry vinegar and gives me a bottle every year or so.

Dijon mustard   For red meat, for adding to salad dressings, for adding sharpness to things that are too sweet, for smearing on ham sandwiches.

FREEZER

Chorizo   My chef brother-in-law Hamish is the person I blame for my chorizo addiction. A few slices fried in a pan (whole, halved or quartered) give a turbo thrust of flavour to soups, roast fennel, braised lentils, roast chicken. The more you use it, the more uses you will find.

Butter   I don't use butter much at all, which is why it stays in the freezer. But there's nothing more annoying than needing it and not having any, and it's easy to cut as much or as little as you need from a frozen block.

Bacon   My friend Steph says there's nothing in life that can't be improved by bacon. I keep around half a kilo of bacon in the freezer at all times, leaving it frozen and simply hacking off as much as I want as I go. Fried bacon lends a luscious smoky note of flavour to everything from braised lentils to casseroles, pasta to risotto, green salad to quiches. (Pork and chicken are the two meats I am inflexibly religious about buying free range, if not organic, for the sake of the animal's quality of life. A great deal of truth-bending goes on in the marketplace and on labels—'bred free range', for example, refers to meat from pigs that were born in a free-range environment but were subsequently raised indoors—so when you find a reliable supplier of true free-range bacon, stock up.)

Parmesan rinds   Keep the ends of parmesan in a bag and toss one in at the beginning of each pot of soup. It only partly melts, and ever so slowly, giving an indefinable richness to vegetable soup.

Pine nuts, hazelnuts, slivered almonds, walnuts, pistachios   Nuts are full of oil, and I learned from Maggie Beer that keeping them in the freezer stops them going rancid and also prevents ruination by pesky pantry moths (if your house is free of these, give thanks). Toasted nuts lend a delightful crunch to dishes like quinoa and couscous that can otherwise tend towards monotony. Lightly bludgeoned pistachios and hazelnuts are wonderful in crumble toppings. I love toasted slivered almonds tossed through rice and in tagines, and pine nuts in a salad still feel like utter luxury. In small quantities, toasted walnuts give robustness and superlative crunch to salads of roast beetroot and feta, and are surprisingly good in salads with strong leaves like spinach or sorrel so long as the dressing is beautifully sweet and acidic. Burned nuts, especially pistachios, are irredeemably horrid. If you burn them, throw them away and learn your lesson.

Almond meal   For the whole orange cake made famous by Claudia Roden, on which there are a million variations (see page 81). For other cakes and slices in place of flour, for frangipane tarts, and to add to fruit crumble toppings.

Chicken stock   Lends flavour to everything—soup, braises (including lentils, of course), risottos, gravies, pasta sauces. Make a huge pot (see page 104) and then decant into containers (yoghurt tubs are good) for freezing. Make sure to include a few tiny containers for when you need only a smidgin.

Breadcrumbs   So as not to waste any precious sourdough. Toast bread ends briefly in the oven and then use a food processor to chop them into rustic lumps. For use as cassoulet or vegetable gratin topping, or tossing through pasta dishes with cauliflower or broccolini and chilli.

Frozen peas   The humble frozen pea, available in every crappy corner shop from here to kingdom come, is one of life's most versatile ingredients. Throw a handful into soups, shepherd's pie, fish curries; braise them with anchovy and mint for a soft, luxurious side dish; add a few to a creamy dressing for cured salmon; toss with chopped prawns through linguine—or make them the star by cooking in stock with softened leeks and shredded lettuce and whiz the lot into a soup of velvety divinity (see page 214).

IN THE FRIDGE
Carrots, celery, onions   Soffrito or mirepoix—nothing more need be said (I find keeping onions cold reduces their tear-inducing

impact when cut—but they soften more quickly this way, so keep the turnover high. I buy two onions every time I shop).

Pomegranate honey   As detailed on page 30, this honey is runnier and less sweet than ordinary honey, and I love the surprise sugar bomb of a pomegranate seed when it pops up in your spoonful of whatever it is. I use pomegranate honey wherever ordinary honey is used, but it only really works with clear, not cloudy, honeys.

Yoghurt   Thick, Greek-style, creamy yoghurt. Toss a spoonful into a fish curry or mix with finely chopped herbs, a little (pomegranate) honey and mustard as a dollopy sauce for grilled fish or barbecued chicken. And use with desserts—sweetened with a little honey if you like—in place of ice-cream or cream.

ON THE BENCH
Olive oil   I buy Australian olive oil in three-litre tins, and refill a brown glass bottle that I keep on the bench. Imported olive oils have been found to have such high levels of adulteration with cheaper vegetable oils, and our home-grown oils are of such comparable if not higher quality, that I'm proud to buy Australian. But oil is spoiled by light and air, so make sure you keep it in a dark-coloured bottle out of the sun, and keep it stoppered. I love those stoppers with a thin spout and a self-closing hinged lid. This is for general cooking—in the pantry is oil for salad dressing.

Salt   A large ceramic tub of cooking salt, and a small one of the lovely pink Murray River flakes.

Garlic   There is only one garlic harvest per crop per year, so even if you buy Australian garlic bulb by bulb, it will all have been harvested at the same time. I buy three or four kilos of organic garlic from www.patricenewell.com each November, and it lasts until around June before it starts to develop long sprouts. We plant some of this, and then resentfully buy imported garlic unless we spot any more local organic stuff in markets or grocers. I have only recently learned that for a long life it is essential to keep garlic dry—which means out of the fridge in a box on the bench, or Patrice's garlic in its beautiful purple box of straw.

At least one orange and two lemons   For the juice, the zest, or whole strips of the skin—a little citrus peel brightens any dish.

Tomatoes   Keep them out of the fridge—coldness ruins the flavour.

IN THE GARDEN (OR POTS ON A WINDOWSILL OR BALCONY)

Woody perennial herbs   Thyme, rosemary, bay leaves, hardy as anything—for stock, soup and slow-braising bases.

Soft annual herbs   Tarragon, basil, parsley, chives, chervil and coriander (when I can get these last two to grow)—for salads, sauces, pasta, curries.

Curry leaves   A hardy, indestructible plant whose fresh leaves are a completely different animal from the dried. I never make a curry without the stunning aromatic pungency of two or three tiny curry leaves. But keep it in a pot—it can run away and become a noxious weed.

Leaves   I am fairly hopeless at vegetable farming, except for leaves— mixed lettuce, lamb's lettuce, beetroot, silverbeet, rocket. A salad of just-picked and washed leaves is a thing of satiny, springy glory. Carefully pick or cut the outer leaves and allow the plant to keep growing. Plant salad seeds or seedlings every few weeks as their growing time is fairly short; lettuce turns bitter as it goes to seed, but you can keep eating the leaves for as long as you find them palatable.

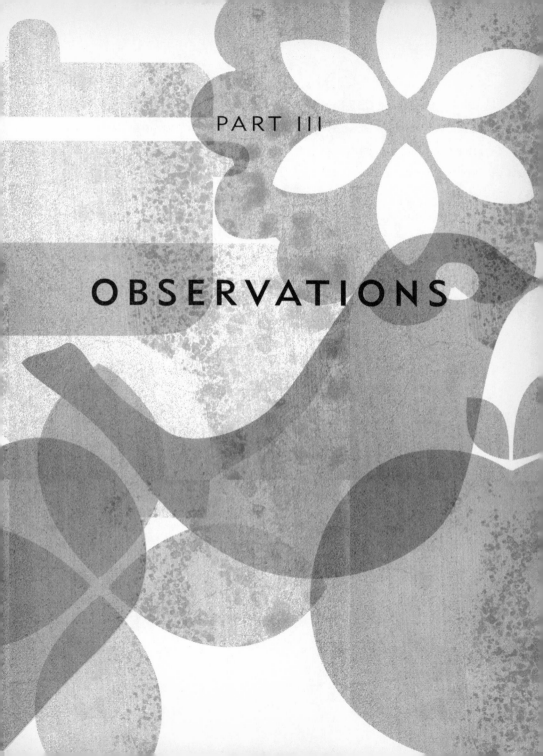

PART III

OBSERVATIONS

LEARNING TO LOVE WHAT YOU HATE: ON PICKY EATING

●

I once shared a few dinners with a woman whose aversion to particular foods bordered on pathological. There were several of us staying at a writers' retreat, and each evening we ate simple meals prepared with great care by an experienced cook. To the rest of the guests the food was unremarkable: mild curries and rice, casseroles, steamed fish, salads. But this woman, whom I shall call Penny, greeted dinnertime with expressions of horror. Peering at a bowl of plain rice, in which a few cardamom pods were dotted, she would say, 'What's that?' Rice, we would answer, nonplussed. 'But it's got *bits* in it!' she cried. 'I can't eat that.' When asked if she had any meal requests, she would cry out: 'Can we have some *normal* food? I like potato!'

Penny was in her fifties, but when it came to mealtimes she might as well have been two and a half. She made pained, disgusted faces at a bowl of minestrone, bending to sniff it, occasionally lifting out a bean or a thread of spinach for inspection: 'What's that stuff?' Offered a piece of rye bread, she flipped it over with a knife, unwilling to touch it. Potato and pasta were okay; herbs or strange vegetables—such as broad beans or, much worse, lentils—were not.

I found myself filling with fury as evening approached, and removed myself from the room as soon as possible after eating, on the pretext of work. Never have I enjoyed mealtimes less.

Years later I remain intrigued not only by Penny's behaviour that week, but by my own irrational anger when faced with it. Why exactly did her carry-on upset me so? For within a day or two it was plain that her behaviour was part of a much larger, sadder problem. Penny was immersed, as she had been for the previous five years, in writing a memoir of childhood abuse. She told me she had read nothing but child-abuse memoirs in those five years. And from her clothes to her body language, her speech patterns—and her food phobias—the lifelong effect of that abuse was plain for all to see. Her experience many decades before at the hands of some predator had made her forever his captive, forever a child.

While Penny's situation was extreme, a similar childishness manifests in much discussion of adult fussiness about food which, it depresses me to learn, is fast becoming known—justifiably or not—as a kind of eating disorder.

Fear of unfamiliar foods is, of course, a perfectly normal part of child development, called neophagia. But many adults, it seems (at least in affluent, Western countries), never get past the kind of food refusal that toddlers are renowned for. A brief search of the internet yields a growing phenomenon of support groups for people who enthusiastically identify as 'Adult Picky Eaters', or APEs. University departments are beginning to study these people, and what causes them to refuse to eat an enormous range of foods. As I read the online comments on the picky-eater discussion boards—*I am so glad to find I am not alone! I have only eaten French fries and saltine crackers for the past fifteen years. I tried to eat a raspberry once but it was so disgusting I threw up*—I find my hackles rising to Penny levels once again.

Perhaps, on closer inspection of these APEs' individual circumstances, as with Penny, I would be forced to get off my high horse and see their disgust as part of a larger syndrome of fear and anxiety. I still don't really understand why defences of such restricted eating, mostly along the lines of 'I wish I could eat an apple, but my body won't let me', aggravate me so much. The bodily response referred to here is vomiting, which we all know to have a deeply psychological component. Who hasn't gagged at the idea of eating certain things? But many of the online APEs appear to be oblivious to the connection between psychology and physical revulsion, and defensive about seeking help to overcome aversions so dire that their relationships and careers are as restricted as the food on their plates.

But why do I find it so enraging? Why on earth do I care what other people put in their mouths, or whether they are missing out on what I consider to be a great deal of pleasure by so restricting their diet? What trespass upon my own beliefs is happening when I witness these responses to food?

Disgust is one of our most primal responses, I discover when I begin to read a little about this. But while it is common to other animals—the 'gape', or gagging reflex, is seen in various other species—the application of that disgust to this or that thing, or food, is very much a learned response.

Imagine my joy when I come across Matthew Brown's fabulously titled essay 'Picky Eating is a Moral Failing' in the collection *Food and Philosophy*. Brown articulates much of what I find so abhorrent about picky eating. (Brown exempts, of course, ethical vegetarians and those with health conditions like gluten intolerance from the picky eater category.) He discusses the issue as a failure of one's moral duty to oneself and to others. The duty to others is easy to articulate: picky eating harms others, Brown says, by inconveniencing them if they are feeding you, and by hurting their feelings when you reject a dish they are offering you. 'When you refuse to share food with others and make it a positive experience, you close off one of the most central ways of connecting with people in everyday life,' he writes. But to me the more interesting part of the essay is that where he argues that picky eating, 'characterised by neophobia, quick judgment, and wilful ignorance', is a violation of the duty to oneself: to develop one's intellectual, emotional, aesthetic and social capacities to their fullest potential.

First, Brown says, one must resist the temptation to draw the conclusion from one bad experience with a certain food that you don't like that food and will never do so. Deciding that because you once ate horrible Brussels sprouts you can never again enjoy the same vegetable is a false premise, showing a closed-mindedness that might easily lead to the habitual refusal of new experiences in other areas of life:

A conscious decision to turn down something unfamiliar and thus a bit frightening at one time becomes a habitual refusal. Decisions become a pattern, and a pattern becomes a habit, and habitual behaviour is done without considering the consequences and can be quite difficult to overcome. And why think that this habit will confine itself to food preference?

I suppose one of the things that most depresses me about the Pennys of the world is how this inflexibility towards food—and I agree with Brown, that it is symptomatic of a much broader attitude of general fear and inflexibility—dooms a person to the same worn rut of experience. Someone who decides that olives are and will always be inedible can never experience the deep delight of looking (or tasting) again, and finding something new and more appealing in the same place. It's this that depresses me so much about the adult picky eaters and their support groups—not just that they have arrested their own development, or even that their extreme revulsion (and in Penny's case, histrionics) curtails any potential pleasure those around them might otherwise take in mealtimes. It's the growing sense of entitlement to what this all means: a claim for closed-mindedness, xenophobia and wilful ignorance; a demand for the social acceptability of eternal childishness.

Carolyn Korsmeyer, another food philosopher who writes fascinatingly about disgust, talks about this when she explains in her essay 'Delightful, Delicious, Disgusting' that the pleasure in sophisticated eating is often predicated on overcoming some initial sense of repulsion. 'Indeed, much of the haute cuisine of a culture retains an element that some people . . . find revolting. And the revulsion appears to be deliberately approached and overcome—not as a matter of necessity, but apparently as a way to increase the depth and potency of taste experience.'

This connection between pleasure and repulsion is not restricted to food, Korsmeyer writes: 'Philosophies of art and aesthetics are peppered with examples of what can be termed the paradox of aversion: the attraction to an object that both inspires fear or revulsion and is transformed into something profoundly beautiful.' She points to the poetic form of tragedy as the most ancient example.

Her point—that it is possible to appreciate and desire something because of the very properties that first repelled one—is not at all difficult to understand for a person who has grown to love oysters.

My first response on tasting an oyster at the age of about twelve was predictable: I spat it out. How on earth anyone could enjoy such a thing—such a cold, slimy, slug-gobbet of a thing—was a mystery to me. And it remained a mystery for many years, as I found it easy to avoid the disgusting grey slugs until my mid-twenties when, bound by the table manners drilled into me by my parents, I found myself at the table of my then-partner's parents, invited to help myself from a platter of oysters. My beau's father loved oysters. To him they were the height of extravagant pleasure, and his offering them to me was a gesture of generosity and warmth. He was inviting me, with this platter of shiny grey slugs, to share his favourite thing. Of course I could not refuse. I took three from the platter, resisting all urgings to take more on the pretext of restraint. I smiled through gritted teeth and prayed I would not retch as I downed them as quickly as possible.

I swallowed the first one whole, forcing myself not to wince. So salty, and so sharp-tasting. But not, I was astonished to find, so disgusting! The second I ate in two bites—amazed to find it interesting. By the third, I had detected the beginnings of what I would soon fall in love with about oysters: the creamy texture, the ice-cold metallic zing. The taste of the ocean, slosh of the water, the grit of sand, the buffeting of the wind. It was incredible. Since that time I've become a fully-fledged oyster-lover—but only because etiquette compelled me to revisit an experience I had absolutely decided I would hate.

FRESHLY SHUCKED OYSTERS

*It was not until I tasted a freshly opened oyster that I truly
begin to love them. A freshly shucked oyster complete with
its little pool of icy sea-juice is a completely different creature
from the pre-opened, dried-out smears of sludge in trays
from the fish shop. I first learned to shuck oysters from a
service-station owner on the south coast of New South Wales,
who sold me a hessian bag of Sydney rocks. He wore a pair
of Stubbies and a welding glove. I took the bag to our beach
campsite and my husband and I somehow opened the lot
using a butter knife. An oyster knife—especially a Dexter
Russell—is much better, and essential if you are going to learn
to love oysters.*

1   Buy a fresh, unopened oyster—I like Sydney rocks best.
2   Hold the oyster firmly on a board with one hand,
    covered by a tea towel to protect it in case you slip,
    with flat side up and the hinge end of the shell
    exposed.
3   Take the oyster knife (I've seen my friend Jane's
    farmer dad use a screwdriver, but wouldn't recom-
    mend it) and dig slowly and firmly into the hinge

part, using a burrowing, gouging motion. Don't try to do it too fast, or use too much force—you'll slip and cut yourself (hence the tea towel; it's best to actually wrap your hand in it until you get better at shucking).

4   Eventually you will feel the knife penetrate the shell; give it a twist and you'll hear a little pop as it opens.

5   Slide the knife along beneath the top shell to release it; once the lid is off, slide the knife beneath the oyster to cut the adductor muscle which attaches the critter to the shell.

6   Flick out any bits of shell, making sure to retain the seawater juices, and rest the opened oyster on a bed of ice for at least 5 or 10 minutes—in my opinion they absolutely must be served chilled! Don't rinse them or lose the briny liquid—it's an essential part of the pleasure. Serve with a squeeze of lemon and sourdough bread.

BRUSSELS SPROUTS WITH BACON

Serves 4

I have never understood why the poor old Brussels sprout is so unfairly maligned. But if you need an incentive to try them again, here I once more invoke Steph's mantra: 'There's nothing in life that can't be improved by bacon.'

250 g Brussels sprouts

3 tablespoons vegetable or peanut oil

2 tablespoons chopped bacon or pancetta

Juice of ½ lemon

Sea salt

1   Steam or boil the sprouts until just tender—about 7 minutes—then drain immediately and halve length-wise, allowing to cool.

2   Heat the oil in a wok or non-stick pan and add bacon; fry until crisp then remove, keeping the bacon fat in the pan.

3   Fry the sprouts gently in the hot bacon fat until very browned, almost charred, but taking care not to mess them around or they will fall apart.

4   Add the lemon juice a little at a time, tasting all the while.

5   Toss sprouts with the bacon pieces and a liberal scatter of salt, and serve.

VEGETARIAN OPTION

Substitute those wonderfully smoky chipotle chillies, soaked and chopped, for bacon.

RHUBARB WITH MAPLE SYRUP AND ORANGE

Serves 4

*Rhubarb was another childhood favourite in our household—
I could never understand why other kids hated it. This recipe
comes from my friend Caro, whose poached rhubarb is the best
I have ever eaten: syrupy, deeply sweet, rosy, dusky, with just a
hint of tartness.*

1 bunch rhubarb
Juice of 1 large or 2 small oranges
1 vanilla bean, scraped
Maple syrup

1   Remove all the leaves and discard—they are
    poisonous—and cut off the flat brown part from the
    end of each stalk.
2   Cut rhubarb into 2.5 cm pieces.
3   Add to a shallow pan with the orange juice, vanilla
    bean and seeds, and a slosh of maple syrup. Stir to
    combine.
4   Simmer gently, stirring occasionally, for 10–12 minutes
    or until rhubarb is tender.
5   Taste the rhubarb; if it's too sour, add more maple
    syrup until it has the sweetness you want.

THE BODY POLITIC:
ON OFFAL AND DISGUST

Once, when I was about nine, our mother cooked us a dinner she refused to name.

'Oh, it's just a white meat,' she said breezily, placing our plates before us on the table. On each plate was a mound of thick white sauce and some stalky parsley. It was a valiant effort on her part, but she was not generally secretive about our dinner. And somehow, once I bit into the springy honeycomb rubber of it, I knew.

'Tripe!' I shrieked, setting off a round of howls among my siblings.

I don't even know how we knew what tripe was, or if I properly tasted it before my outburst, but I recall the meal so particularly because it was one of the two occasions as children we were permitted not to eat what was in front of us. Even my parents threw theirs in the bin that evening. (The other time involved a bread-and-butter pudding made for us by a neighbour. For the life of me I can't think what she must have done to it, but it was so revolting that, four decades on, nobody in my family has ever eaten that dessert by choice since.)

I love all kinds of meat but I have always been squeamish about offal. Liver, kidneys, brains—I have managed to avoid eating these, purely on psychological grounds, all of my life. But that's not quite true. In fact I have occasionally enjoyed offal—but only when it bore no visual resemblance to itself, and I could manage to turn my mind from what it was. My friend Stephanie Clifford-Smith, a food writer and peerless culinary adventuress, reminds me that in her company I have tucked into a Laotian salad of shredded tripe, along with some grilled slices of tongue. I remember the tongue because, though I found the first slice delicious, the sight of it neatly arranged in its perfect tongue shape on the plate was simply too much and I couldn't face any more. Another time, though, Steph reminds me, I ate crunchy, fried pig's intestines buried under a mountain of dried chilli in a Chinese restaurant. After my initial hesitation, she recalls, I ate with gusto.

If I feel any disquiet about my relationship to meat in general, it's on ethical grounds to do with the suffering of animals and the environmental destruction caused by meat production. But I have no bodily aversion to eating animal flesh, and in fact I love the taste and texture of it. So why am I repulsed by the thought of eating an animal's organs?

Perhaps the greatest challenge to my view of myself as a sophisticated eater was experienced on a trip to China. In the markets, the streets and the restaurants, one is constantly confronted with evidence of just how removed we squeamish Westerners are from the death of animals we eat. In Shanghai, where I have visited my sister-in-law Kate and her husband Hamish Pollitt, ducks are slaughtered to order on the street, live eels stripped using nothing more than a nail, and the feet and faces of pigs and goats displayed along with their haunches in butcher shops. In a wet market where we ordered a chicken, the bird moved from feathered clucking life to plucked and cleavered death within a minute. I turned my horrified gaze from the moment of the death, which occurred instantaneously and without fuss. Where Australians prefer their meat faceless, skinless and generally as visually divorced as possible from the fact of the animal's death, the Chinese harbour no such qualms. Eating meat involves death. To pretend otherwise is indulgent, laughable.

The Chinese devotion to offal, too, is legendary. Thanks to Hamish, executive chef at Shanghai's famous M on the Bund restaurant, I recently found myself invited to a private staff supper, a dining experience unlike any other I've ever had.

We arrived at the private rooms in a Shanghainese restaurant in a corporate-looking building high above the city at about 11.30 pm, after service at M had finished. My husband and I found ourselves in a dining room thick with smoke, seated at a huge round table among three Australian and twenty or so Shanghainese chefs and kitchen hands, all ready to cut loose after several extraordinarily busy months in the restaurant.

Amid cries of *Gambei!* and the hurling back of shots of *baijiu*—the 55 per cent proof Chinese spirit liquor I had tasted once before and knew I must politely decline if I were to remain vertical—the food began to arrive.

I was keen to show my appreciation at being present; not only was I the only woman at an occasion usually reserved for men, but their generosity in inviting a pair of strangers to share their private party was something we appreciated very much. As well, with someone else footing the bill, the staff would have no hesitation in ordering expensive delicacies that might ordinarily be unaffordable. I would be seeing and tasting food here that I might never have the opportunity to eat again.

Good manners, then, demanded—even more than usual—that I eat from every dish offered to me. This is the kind of occasion when the squeamish can offer a silent prayer of gratitude to the inventor of the lazy Susan; helping yourself means the possibility for small taste tests and the avoidance of anything too overwhelmingly confronting to eat.

It was a salutary and very simple lesson in overcoming disgust: all I had to do was refrain from asking what something was until after I'd tasted it. So later, once some of the most delicate, pungent and texturally sumptuous food I had ever eaten had passed my lips, I learned that I had partaken of lungs, intestines, tongues and livers, as well as a kind of overpoweringly scented (some might less generously describe it as a stench) fermented tofu Hamish fondly calls 'Chinese gorgonzola'.

Nobody really noticed what I ate, and I was not forced to eat anything that truly offended my tastebuds or stomach. But in overcoming my own small prejudices I was able to properly accept the generosity of the invitation, and more fully experience an evening I will remember all my life.

Back home, bothered by the sheer illogic of it, I began to think about why and how powerfully my mind works against the possibility of enjoying offal. For I could not so freely enter into judgement of others for their picky eating while ignoring the presence of my own nonsensical aversions. How much difference is there between my abhorrence of offal and someone else's hatred of rhubarb? Both, surely, involve the same decision to close one's mind, shutting down the possibility that a previously unpleasant experience could at another time be found bearable or even pleasurable. If I think a refusal to eat rhubarb is childish and limits one's potential to grow into an open-minded, fully rounded human being, how can I justify not eating a heart or a lung? What is going on, in the deeper recesses of my mind, that I don't quite understand?

A little reading confirms my hunch that an aversion to the internal organs of animals taps into darker fears than mere dislike. It seems my feelings of revulsion in this matter fit like a glove into what psychologist and world-renowned 'disgust' researcher Paul Rozin calls the basic emotion of 'core disgust'. My revulsion has nothing to do with disliking the taste, or any other physical, sensory factor—it's purely psychological. And the idea of eating what I can visually identify as *body parts*, rather than more generalised 'meat', evokes a primal response. Rozin claims that humans, and I expect most especially we affluent Westerners, are disgusted by anything that reminds us of the fact of our own animal bodies.

'Humans see themselves as quite distinct from (and superior to) other animals,' he has written, 'and wish to avoid any ambiguity about their status by accentuating the human–animal boundary.'

When we look at animals, however, we are forced to see what we most obviously have in common with them: the basic bodily functions of breathing, eating, defecating—and dying. When I contemplate the dead cow's tongue lying on its bed of lettuce in the Laotian restaurant, at some deep level, Rozin and his colleagues believe, I am forced to contemplate my own animal tongue—and my own death. I reject this contemplation immediately, unconsciously, by rejecting the tongue itself.

'The most threatening aspect of humans' animalness is their mortality,' Rozin says, 'and that disgust serves as a defence against pondering mortality.'

So what is happening here is simple, ancient and powerful: fear of death.

I can easily accept this theory—and perhaps another idea too: the sort of psychic disruption that occurs when (in this breach of the body envelope Rozin describes), what should remain *inside* is brought out—as the origins of my revulsion.

In light of all this, in the interests of experimentation, and in the hope that understanding might bring acceptance, I decided to try cooking offal for myself. I wanted to test these fears of mine, to see exactly how strong was my aversion to handling, cooking and eating offal—and whether my squeamishness was purely psychological or did have something to do with taste and texture after all.

I chose tripe (the lining of an animal's stomach—in this case, cow), the childhood symbol of my offal hysteria. Adulthood has shown me many other examples of how better cooking can transform previously disliked foods into favourites, after all. And if the Italians love tripe, smothered in tomato, garlic, parsley and so on, how bad could it be? Further, I decided that tripe could surely be no more squidgy and bouncy and rubbery than squid or octopus, both of which I love, and must be bland enough in flavour to allow the sauce to mask any creepiness of taste.

So I tried Stephanie Alexander's 'beginner' tripe recipe—tripe with tomato and lots of parsley—which she describes as a blend of French and Italian traditions. 'If you don't like this,' Alexander writes, 'you don't like tripe.'

I expected the first obstacle to be handling the meat, but was surprised to find it quite lovely to touch. A piece of bleached tripe is a pretty little pouch—a kind of soft, frilly sea sponge.

In the cooking, I decided to pretend the tripe was squid—both as a textural guide and to start bending my resistant mind to the possibility of eating it—and was hoping for a similar texture once cooked to tenderness. A friend confirmed that well-cooked tripe should have a little resistance to the tooth and then be slippery and springy.

I cooked the tripe for a little over an hour in the delicious tomato sauce, then topped it with parmesan and set it under the grill for a few minutes as Alexander suggests.

Then came the big moment. I tried a piece, and found it revoltingly springy and chewy, though it was tender enough. What was fascinating to observe was how it was my *mind* that caused the problem. With every chew, my mind screamed: *Stomach Lining! Quivery Slimy Thing! Animal Innards! DEATH!*

I tried again, finding a much smaller piece, with lots of sauce, far easier to contemplate. In this way, and by focusing hard on imagining how my mind would be working if this were squid—*Springy!*

Delicious! Tender! Lovely surprising texture!—I chomped happily away on a small ramekin full of tripe. Yes, there was a very slight echo of unusual flavour, so slight as to almost be attributable to my imagination. And yes, the frills added a textural frisson that might take some getting used to. But all in all, it was completely fine.

I'm not sure how often I will cook tripe again—if ever—but I found the exercise satisfying. For now, if I visited your house and you served me a huge bowlful of tripe, I would no longer stiffen in terror and allow my stomach to flip over itself in panic and revulsion. And who knows, on another tasting or two I might find, as I have done with so many foods since childhood, from chilli to muesli to oysters, that it grows on me and I begin to like it very much.

ON HUNGER

'Think of the children starving in Africa.'

I don't actually recall this classic rebuke ever being said to me or my siblings, possibly because my memories of childhood and food are more about a kind of anxious greediness rather than refusing what was on the plate. I know this can't be entirely true, because I do have the odd, singular image of sitting alone in a cold kitchen, engaged in some kind of standoff with a vegetable long after everyone else had left the table. It was the era when children were not involved in discussion about what or how much to eat, and to the best of my recollection any attempt by a child to reject food in our house was cheerfully ignored.

As a family, in fact, I think we were a fairly gluttonous lot. Let's just say the concept of 'mindful eating'—of paying close attention to the textures, aromas, appearance and taste of every mouthful as you slowly savour it—never made it to 4 Goonda Street, Cooma North, during the 1970s. Second helpings were de rigueur, but only if you were fast enough. Any mindfulness was applied to the size rather than the quality of each mouthful. Gluttony was no sin; it was a way of life. My parents' Catholicism leaned more towards social justice than the superstitious hocus-pocus peddled by the nuns and priests at school, so the talk of hell and sin that went on in my friends' homes was never heard in ours. But it does seem a little curious to me now that in a home otherwise so dominated by ideas about social responsibility and one's duty to others, restraint where food was concerned never entered anyone's head.

Despite this generally approved gluttony (or, I wonder now, because of it?), the world's starving children nevertheless had a strong, if ghostly, presence in my childhood. Perhaps I was a particularly ghoulish sort of child, but images of potbellied African children or raggedly-dressed Indian urchins seem a familiar motif in my early memories. I have a particularly strong memory of the purple cardboard World Vision collection box that seemed always to sit on a corner of the kitchen bench, with its black and white photographs of suffering children and its coin slot for donations.

My mother's brother lived in Kathmandu for much of his adult life; he helped to set up a Sherpa cooperative trekking company and lived there until he died at fifty-nine. When I grew up I loved his irascible disavowal of worldly goods and his dedication to a life lived simply alongside his Nepalese friends, and I feel proud to have had such a radical gent as an uncle. But in primary school, during Uncle Michael's occasional visits to us, I was insulted by his rudeness about the pathetic size of our beloved Snowy Mountains. Worse, I found his lack of desire for material goods embarrassing. I hated his lectures to us children about how lucky we were, how affluent we were, how many Nepalese families could live for a month on the cost of a pair of sneakers I coveted.

When he returned to Nepal, now and then a battered brown paper parcel would arrive, bearing exotic gifts that we admired and feared in equal measure. I loved a picture book about one boy's search for the Abominable Snowman of Mount Everest—the book was illustrated with photographs of a real Nepali boy, visiting temple monkeys and street vendors to ask them how he could find the mythological man. The boy was healthy-looking enough, though his clothes were rags. But the other gifts were less accessible: heavy, sharp brass ornaments for girls to wear in their hair, or thick, scratchy rugs made from coarse animal hair. The gift I detested the most was a goatskin cap. For a nine-year-old girl who longed only for an acrylic beanie in Eastern Suburbs rugby league team colours like her friends', it would be difficult to find a more humiliating garment to be forced to wear walking to school than this greasy brown leather cap—with fleece-lined *earflaps*, if you please. I hated that hat not only for its ugliness, but for what it represented. It smelled sourly of goat and a kind of smoky foreignness. It was the smell of third-world poverty, and I hated it.

Another spectre of foreign suffering was delivered to us through an obscure charity that our mother was involved with throughout our childhoods. To this day the Ryder-Cheshire Foundation continues to care for the most vulnerable people in India—those with intellectual disabilities and 'burnt out leprosy patients', according to its website. One of the foundation's more curious fund-raising activities when I was a child was the sale of small vinyl-covered notebook diaries.

Perfectly ordinary diaries, except for the fact they were heavily illustrated throughout with black and white photographs of the lepers. I'm not sure how old I was when I was so taken with these diaries (each one had a teeny little pencil that fitted pleasingly into the spine), but I recall a period of childhood during which I would steal away into a quiet corner with one and peer, it seemed for hours, at the stumps and bandages, the stick-thin limbs and toothless grimaces of these legless, armless creatures.

There were also other, more pointed activities to direct our attention to starvation. One of these involved a gathering for dinner at our school hall on a Saturday night—but instead of dinner you were given what an African family would reputedly eat for theirs: a small bowl of plain rice. I recall little about this event except my sense of utter outrage. I had to eat this! *Rice.* I don't think my disgust was so much about the rice itself (although I can't help but point out how revoltingly soggy it would have been; no white people seemed to know how to cook rice back then), as much as the fact of being forced to consider, with my own body, the suffering that complete strangers were enduring in foreign lands. I was ten, and I didn't want to know.

Now I'm forty-five, and I still don't want to know.

What I mean is that, like most people, I am uncomfortable with the obscenity of my wealth; with the fact that I have so much food of such high quality, while millions are slowly dying from starvation.

The British restaurant critic AA Gill entered the heart of this obscenity when he went to Africa to report on the 'hunger gap' in South Sudan. In his searing essay 'The End of the Road', he describes what he saw there in clear, unsentimental prose. He tells of his shock at receiving a smile of welcome, the offer of a drink of water, from the starving Dinka people. When it came time to sit and eat with the field workers of Médecins Sans Frontières, he writes: 'I was dreading dinner: how do you eat in a promise of famine? Actually, it is not difficult; not to eat would be a silly act of self-mortification.' He and the MSF workers ate muesli bars and sandwiches while, on the other side of a row of thorn bushes, 'the starving stood and watched'.

This, writ large, is what most of us do three times a day: eat well in the presence, at some level, of the starving. But one is wary of the self-mortification Gill describes. Is even discussing starvation in a book about food and pleasure an act of self-indulgence? And if it is, how then is one to behave?

For most of us in Australia—in 2008 reported as the fattest nation in the world—the physical sensation of hunger is so foreign we actually fail to recognise it. A nutritionist once told me that a significant part of her job involves describing what hunger feels like: the stomach does rumble, there may be a mild pain in the stomach, you might feel lightheaded, distracted or—my favourite—you may feel increasingly angry. And, she said, the contemporary practice of allowing children to 'graze' all day—neither forced to eat what they are given, nor to wait until mealtimes to eat anything—means they will never experience what hunger or satiety feel like.

But you don't have to be a child to have forgotten what it is to be hungry.

I can remember the last time I craved food from bodily need rather than mere desire. It was two years ago, at the end of a day in which I shovelled and wheelbarrowed several tonnes of sand and earth from a heap in the street into my back yard. I remember the deep and simple exhaustion that followed my eight hours of hard physical labour, and the curious pleasure of Being Hungry.

But for most of my days, deskbound and never far from food, I eat to alleviate boredom or to distract myself. In our culture, we dramatise 'being hungry' into an almost unthinkable emergency. The writer Joanne Fedler speaks of this tendency in her book *When Hungry, Eat*, describing how her mother always insisted she take a banana in her bag 'in case you get hungry', reinforcing the idea that natural, ordinary hunger is something to be prevented at all costs, something to be feared and loathed. The idea that growing hungry is a normal, healthy part of life—a sensation we should be able to manage for at least a few hours without going into emotional crisis—is completely foreign to a society drowning in advertising for snack foods. When you think about it, a whole category of foods to eat while you're waiting to eat is really very strange.

Only when I deliberately lost weight not long ago did I learn that for several hours at least, it is possible for feelings of hunger to come *and go,* that it is possible for me not to obsess and fall into panic at the first sign of a rumbling tummy. I was shocked at how little I understood the fact that hunger is an altogether different sensation from *not being full.*

In a society where *The Biggest Loser* and *MasterChef* are screened in an endless cycle of denial and panic followed by excess and panic followed by more denial and more panic, I sometimes find it difficult to believe that an abiding interest in food is not at least a little obscene, and a lot trivial.

British philosopher Elizabeth Telfer explores this problem in her book *Food for Thought*. She examines our obligations to help alleviate the hunger and suffering of others, and our simultaneous right to pursue a good life for ourselves. After detailing the obvious ways we could help others—giving away all we do not need and diverting those funds to the alleviation of hunger—she explores the position that there is a limit to our moral duty towards others. 'We have a right to some things that are immune to the claims of others,' she writes, later adding: 'We have not merely a right but a duty to cultivate our talents, develop ourselves and do what is valuable in itself—in other words, to pursue the worthwhile life.'

I find myself overwhelmingly relieved to read these words, for I sincerely believe my interest in food and its web of connections to other people and new ideas and experiences does indeed help to make my life worthwhile. And yet I am not completely convinced. Is it merely lapsed-Catholic guilt that makes me feel too easily let off the hook by this? I would like to wholeheartedly embrace Telfer's position—that my moral duty to myself is as powerful as my duty to others—but find it difficult to resist the idea that this is too neat, too simple.

All this may, of course, be too indulgently guilt-stricken, self-flagellating—especially, as I have already said, in a book about cooking. Get over yourself, I can hear more than one of you muttering. But then I recall the questions posed by David Foster Wallace in his beautiful contemplation of the rights of crustaceans, 'Consider the Lobster', published in *Gourmet* magazine in 2004. After considering whether the lobsters at the Maine Lobster Festival feel pain, or suffer, Foster Wallace addresses those who might read his words as 'just so much pointless navel-gazing'.

'After all,' he writes, 'isn't being extra aware and attentive and thoughtful about one's food and its overall context part of what distinguishes a real gourmet? Or is all the gourmet's extra attention and sensibility just supposed to be aesthetic, gustatory?'

I am left to conclude that, as with most matters of ethics, how much I am obliged to worry about this is a matter of degree, and of motive. And I must find my own way.

If I resist the fetishisation of food for its own sake, if I contribute a reasonable proportion of my income to organisations working against hunger, if I curb my tendency to thoughtlessly overeat, if I keep thinking about where my own personal line between pleasure and excess lies, if I use cooking and an appreciation of food in a way that develops my own intellectual and emotional capacities, and connects me to others . . . If I do these things mindfully, and without forgetting, then perhaps it could be acceptable to eat while the starving watch.

FAMILIAR THINGS NEW: THE ELEMENT OF SURPRISE

I have come to think that one of the marks of an excellent cook, as opposed to the rest of us, is the former's talent for surprise.

It's the same with writing. What pleases me first as a reader is the feeling that I'm in completely safe hands—at times I think this is the aspect of reading that gives me the most pleasure of all: a writer's control of their material, their effortless-seeming blend of form and content to create something seamless, something beautiful. It's a kind of beauty that has nothing to do with the story itself, but everything to do with its construction.

But it's the element of surprise that takes literary appreciation to a higher plane for me, always. It might be the tiniest unexpected thing—an unusual but perfectly precise image, a striking cadence, or an observation so acute it jolts you into seeing the world afresh. I believe it was Samuel Johnson who said the most engaging skill of a writer is that 'new things are made familiar, and familiar things are made new'.

But surprise for its own sake brings no pleasure for me—not in something to read nor something to eat. The kind of novel with wildly eccentric plots spanning eighteen centuries, characters who turn from dogs into Martians into piano accordions, or other such startling measures designed to make a reader sit up, bug-eyed with admiration, are not for me.

In the same way, a restaurant with a menu whose main objective is to startle is very rarely a place I want to visit.

I was once lucky enough to be taken by my brother-in-law Bernard to Heston Blumenthal's restaurant The Fat Duck in Bray, England. It was one of the most gorgeously outlandish evenings of my life. I tasted the astonishment that is his famous bacon-and-egg ice-cream, and swooned. It was heavenly, and so joyously silly (it came with a serving of 'parsnip-flake' cereal in a little box, just like the mini-boxes of Coco Pops in bad hotels) I almost fell off my chair with the pleasure of it. But Heston Blumenthal is a magician, his food is sublime in texture, flavour and appearance, and his restaurant is a theatre of the absurd. Other performers of his ilk, like Ferran Adrià—whose renowned restaurant elBulli closed its doors in 2011—I am happy to admire from afar.

It's not their fault, but Blumenthal and Adrià have spawned a whole species of copycat restaurants where the food is ridiculous, and entirely lacking in their subtlety and skill. These are the kind of places where the chef either shoves bizarre ingredients together in an effort to impress, or mangles every dish into pretentiousness with an added smear of pond scum.

In the first category lies the expensive restaurant in which a friend—against his better judgement but to satisfy his curiosity—ordered 'fillet of beef with banana'. He was intrigued to see what magical transformation would take place in flavour and texture. There was none. The banana simply sat, a log, on top of the steak.

In the second category falls a regional molecular gastronomy restaurant another friend once visited. At this place the food included something called 'an interim of parsley dust', served by po-faced staff so taken with their cult leader, the chef, that they were too frightened to bring my friend some salt when she pointed out the underseasoning of her cauliflower macaron.

This could just be funny, except the food costs two hundred dollars, you leave drunk and starving, and the whole point seems intimidation rather than charm. It's less surprise, more ambush, designed to distance the diner from the food and its creator by a calculated jolt into unfamiliarity. And there you are, stranded with your carrot air and your liquorice paint, and the message is clear: be impressed or go home.

It seems to me Blumenthal is coming from somewhere else entirely. His whacky ice-cream seems designed to provoke a teasingly delightful confusion of the senses. It's like being spun round, blindfolded, but with safe, warm hands to catch you should you topple. This interplay of the familiar and unfamiliar—the impish breakfast motifs included—has the effect of drawing you and the food's creator together into a light and joyful game.

It's only since I began work on this book that I have come to realise how similar are my approaches to creating and consuming both food and literature. I am happiest when both things are motivated by the same desire EM Forster articulated in his famous injunction: 'Only connect!' It is in this connection, I think, that the proper motive for surprise lies—to delight rather than impress, to draw people closer, to join rather than separate.

The best cooks I know give quite simple foods an unexpected layer or twist—with an ingredient, a technique, or some other modest surprise. The following list includes nothing outlandish, but these tiny additions—some of which I have enthused about already—are the things our dinner guests most love and ask about when they taste them.

Currants　Small and sweet and surprising, a handful of currants (perhaps plumped first in vinegar) added to a tagine, a bowl of fragrant rice, a couscous or quinoa or simple green salad, is a lovely thing.

Orange or mandarin peel　A slow-cooked dish which has included a curl of orange or mandarin skin has a sweet, sombre earthiness. It is like the beauty of a low piano chord that you only notice after you tire of the surface melody.

Maple syrup and tamari　The Australian-British cook Skye Gyngell has made this sweet and salty combination her signature, and it is excellent. The more often you add a spoonful of each to meat dishes, stocks and dressings, the more places you will find to use it.

Porcini mushrooms   Another earthy echo of flavour—use some plumped porcini wherever you use other kinds of mushrooms, or add them chopped to roast chicken pan juices, risotto or soup.

Labneh   The silky soft texture of labneh (see page 31) and its delicately acidic flavour is a delightful combination. Add to a bowl of spicy vegetable soup, any type of Indian curry, or scatter through a leaf salad with some cooked Puy lentils.

Chorizo   Another ingredient you can find endless uses for once you begin. Fry thin rounds of chorizo and then add them whole or quartered to thick vegetable soups, strong-leaved salads of spinach or rocket, or throw a few into poultry roasts and braises. Some chorizo flung into a pan of roasting fennel is a fine thing.

Caraway seeds   Such a bright, surprising, toasty flavour and fine, indefinable crunch. Caraway is delicious in bread and cheese biscuits, and also, most obviously, with cabbage. But I find I increasingly want to put it with orange things—roasted carrots and pumpkin, with orange juice in dressings and sauces.

Walnut oil   I may be easily pleased, but I find a salad dressing with an unexpected flavour a joyful thing. Walnut oil is strongly flavoured, so using half and half walnut and olive oil in a salad dressing is very good, as is a thread drizzled over a punchy bean soup.

Raspberry vinegar   Another contender for the surprising salad dressing. Sweet and sharp, real raspberry vinegar is syrupy and luscious if used in dressings, to plump dried fruit, or added by the thimbleful to anything that tastes a little flat or dull.

Pomegranate   I have the Ottolenghi chefs to thank for my love of the pomegranate, with its astonishing sweet-and-sour crunch. Few things are more aesthetically pleasing than the glassy rubies of pomegranate seeds sprinkled through a pale-looking salad, or added to a tagine, or piled high on an orange cake. Pomegranate molasses, used sparingly, is excellent in dressings, and I use my pomegranate honey (see page 30) in place of ordinary honey. My friend Jane showed me that a few seeds of pomegranate dropped into a glass of sparkling wine provide hours of amusement—they zoom up and down the glass like tiny ruby submarines.

Chermoula   A paste of spices and herbs so full of flavour that even just a spoonful provides an electric jolt of energy. Make up your own from coriander root, stem and leaves, chilli, onion, a little oil and spices galore, and keep it in the freezer. I add a lump to soups, or rub it over meats before barbecuing, or use it to marinate fish, or coat vegetables in it before roasting.

Chipotle   The nearest thing to vegetarian bacon I have found. This Mexican smoke-dried jalapeno chilli is wonderful when plumped in water or vinegar and added to soups or casseroles, stir-fried with brussels sprouts (see page 145), combined with lentils and chickpeas, or generally used anywhere you might otherwise fling bits of bacon.

Nuts   I find something crunchy in an otherwise soft mouthful is always pleasing. Slivered almonds in couscous or rice dishes, chopped walnuts in a spinach salad with a sweetish dressing, hazelnuts in a fruit crumble topping, toasted pine nuts with roasted cauliflower, cashews in a chickpea curry; nuts can make simple food sublime.

PART IV

CONSOLATIONS

YOU STILL HAVE TO EAT

Seventeen years ago, when my two youngest sisters were caring for our sick mother at home, twice a week a neighbour called Ruby would come knocking at their door.

'How's ya mum, darlin?' she would croak. 'Doin any bedda today?'

Ruby was aged around eighty, about four feet tall, and as slight as a stick. She had a smoker's voice so gloriously raspy she might have roughened it daily on a carpenter's rasp. The weathered skin of her face was grey with lack of oxygen and the fact she walked anywhere, let alone up our mother's three front steps, seemed heroic.

No, the girls would have to tell Ruby, our mother was still not feeling so good. Sometimes they would lie and say that she was feeling a bit perkier today, or had some colour in her cheeks, was up to eating. It seemed too sad to answer Ruby's hopeful questions with the truth: that our mother was dying. But what the girls said really made no difference; no matter their response, Ruby would shake her head.

'Ah, the poor bugger,' she'd say, wheezing soulfully at the doormat. Then, as she did every visit, she would make her offering. 'Just a bit of sumthink for ya mum, darlin, to make her feel better.'

Every time, my sisters would exclaim and accept Ruby's offering with gratitude. Then she would hobble off down the garden path until the next visit.

Ruby's bits of something really were quite something. The gift always came in one small, speckled ceramic cereal bowl, covered in slightly sodden cling wrap. In the bowl was always some bizarre concoction. A few sardines wrapped in a slice of devon, perhaps, or three little sippets of white toast with baked beans, given a glossy slipcover of condensed milk, or a thick slab of undercooked scone dough fashioned into a lumpy pineapple-and-Vegemite pizza.

I can't accurately recall all of Ruby's dishes, but tapioca, arrow-root, sago and junket seem to feature in my memory, usually in strong-smelling combination with other treats—fricasseed brains, maybe, or tuna mornay.

Of course, in our small town Ruby's gifts of solace were just a few among many. A casserole appeared on the doorstep for my sisters at least once or twice a week over those months, most often without a note or anything else to identify the giver. It was the kind of routine kindness that happened then in country towns and suburbs everywhere.

A decade before this, our father, too, was gravely ill. Back then our mother was just forty-eight years old, bewildered with shock and grief, and trying to come to terms with this hole punched in our world while caring for a houseful of equally stunned teenagers.

One day, a ute appeared in our driveway. Someone unloaded a small chest freezer and installed it in our kitchen. It was packed to the brim with frozen casseroles, soups, pies and desserts. For the many months of treatment and grieving that followed, that freezer was restocked every week by neighbours and friends.

That year on Christmas Day, as every day, we went to visit our dad in hospital.

Our neighbours then were Jim and Pat Rodda and their kids. The Roddas had lived next door forever and we loved them nearly as much as our own family. We had never heard of Jim cooking before, but at lunchtime that day we came home to find our dining table spread with a lavish Christmas feast—turkey, ham and all the trimmings—that Jim had cooked for us entirely by himself.

The food was excellent, but the gift was far more serious than that. Though he and our dad were chalk and cheese—Jim drank beer and adored golf more than life itself, while our eccentric father spent his time reading Catholic theology and making wine from oak leaves and raisins—they loved each other. And of course Jim was a father himself. It was only much later that I understood the magnitude of his cooking for us that day. It was not so much a present for us, but a message to our father, an expression of masculine love and fatherly solidarity that to this day makes me cry to think of it. Our dad died the next day, taking with him the knowledge that his family would be cared for by our town in exactly such tender, graceful ways.

These things—Ruby's alarming concoctions, the freezer full of casseroles and Jim's Christmas dinner—all happened a long time ago, when my siblings and I were very young people. But the experience went deep. Now, for all of us, when news of a friend's or neighbour's crisis hits, our first instinct is: cook.

I used to think this impulse was common to everyone, not just people raised in country towns. Perhaps it was usual at one time. But I have come to think we've lost confidence in our instincts. Recently, I heard that one of our neighbours was having cancer treatment, and had been for several months. I felt dreadful that we'd not known, and had done nothing for his wife and kids before now, so my husband and I popped round with a quiche. It wasn't much, obviously—more a gesture than anything—but still, I trusted my instincts.

When V. opened the door I was shocked. Not because she looked any different—she didn't, except perhaps a little tired, for her husband was in hospital again, this time with pneumonia. But as she took the quiche from us she began to cry, and said this was the first time anyone had done such a thing. Her gratitude was completely over the top—it was only a quiche—but it made me remember how magnified the smallest gestures of kindness can become when one is marooned in this way by terror and grief. And it made me ashamed, that our neighbours had been left alone with it for so long.

How does this happen? I wonder if it might partly have to do with our contemporary preoccupation with experts, and outsourcing, and privacy. In middle-class Australia, it seems that if something—especially the most intimate of human needs—needs addressing, it is always possible to pay a stranger to do it. From the washing of undies to the cleaning of one's toilet, from the mending of a broken heart to insomnia or nightmares, from toenail clipping to hair removal, these days one need never turn to one's family or friends for help in caring for one's ailing body or soul.

In general I find this enormously liberating. Who wants to assault one's friends with yet another round of howling over a lover's betrayal, or the details of that (let's face it, unpleasant) intimate medical issue? Professional help, if affordable, is a fine thing, allowing the maintenance of one's dignity and privacy in matters of the heart or hoof.

And yet. I think of Ruby, and the freezer, and Jim, and my neighbour dissolving in tears over a bacon-and-egg quiche. And these incidents reinforce what I already know: food is not just food, and cooking is not just a practical act. A casserole on the doorstep can be nourishment not only to the body—which is essential—but also an act of love, a refreshment for the mind and the soul. When things are too terrible to talk about, an offering of home-cooked food is a silent, loving letter telling your broken-hearted friend or your ailing aunt that they are not alone, that someone cares, that they are loved.

There is one more incident I've remembered. My friend Paul, an excellent cook, was devastated to learn of the serious illness of a family friend who himself had a young family. Paul came up with the obvious way to help: he would deliver a weekly meal to the family home without fuss, without intrusion. He rang the friend's wife to make his offer, relieved he had finally found a practical way to help. Her response was unexpected. No thank you, she said icily. She was not a charity case, his social work was not required, and he should find someone else to patronise. Paul, of course, was mortified. Not only had he not found a way to help, he had made things much, much worse.

This is a dreadful story but it's rare. To my mind the story only shows that the woman was in a state of such grief that she could not respond to kindness. Which brings me to realise that there is more than one gift happening when you offer a dish of food: the gracious acceptance of it is a gift in return. What my sisters did every time they took one of Ruby's pineapple-and-Vegemite pizzas was let her know that her kindness was helping them, and it did. The food may have been inedible, but the love in it was one of the many acts of simple humanity that sustained those young women through six months of caring for a dying mother.

Just as importantly, offerings like Ruby's taught us how to do the same (with a few adjustments!) for someone else. In *The Gift*, Lewis Hyde's much-loved book on creativity, Hyde says one of the most important things about gifts is that they must be kept in motion.

'Whatever we have been given is supposed to be given away again, not kept . . . In fact, it is better if the gift is not returned but is given instead to some new, third party. The only essential is this: the gift must always move.'

If your gift is refused, there is nothing to be done but mark it down to experience. But I can guarantee that there are far many more neighbours who will be grateful for the smallest plate of home-cooked food than there are those who might lash out at the offer. Amazingly, most human beings intuitively understand—even in the depths of their despair—that the gift must always move.

So, to anyone who has ever heard of a friend in need and thought, 'I wish there was something I could do to help,' there is. It's called chicken cacciatore or lamb tagine or couscous with pine nuts or *soupe au pistou* or beef Bourguignon or *linguine al pesto*. It's also called, simply, love.

Florence Nightingale soup

Serves 6

When my friend Di's sister died, a big pot of this green-and-white chicken noodle soup kept her going for several days. Inspired by Karen Martini's chicken brodo recipe, I have also found it to cure many ills of body and spirit.

1.5 kg chicken wings

Olive oil

2 litres chicken stock

1 bunch silverbeet, stems finely chopped, leaves cut into
   strips

1 leek, finely chopped

1 small or ½ large fennel bulb, finely chopped

5 cloves garlic, finely chopped

1 cup white cabbage, finely chopped

2 celery sticks, finely chopped

1 carrot, finely chopped

½ cup arborio rice

50 g spaghetti, broken into 5 cm sticks

Handful green beans, chopped into 2 cm lengths

2 zucchinis, sliced

½ cup cauliflower, broken into small florets

½ cup frozen peas

½ bunch parsley, chopped, to serve

Salt and pepper

1   Toss the wings in olive oil with lots of salt and roast at 220°C until golden (about 20 minutes).

2   Bring stock to the boil. Toss in chicken wings and cook on a rolling boil for another 20 minutes.

3   Turn off heat, remove wings from stock and leave to cool.

4   Meanwhile, in a heavy-based pan fry silverbeet stems, leek, fennel, garlic, cabbage, celery and carrot over high heat until they begin to turn golden.

5   This is the fiddly part. When wings are cool enough, pick off the meat and discard bones and half the skin, leaving a little bowl of deliciously moist shreds of chicken.

6   Bring stock to the boil again, and throw in the rice, then add the pasta a few minutes later.

7   Add the sautéed vegetables, then the remaining vegetables.

8   Season well and cook until everything is tender, giving the soup a stir now and then to make sure nothing sticks.

9   Add the parsley and check the seasoning.

Spinach Quiche

Serves 6

1 quantity frozen shortcrust pastry or rough puff pastry
    (see page 91)
Olive oil
1 bunch silverbeet, washed, stems and leaves separated and
    finely chopped
1 onion, finely chopped
3 tablespoons chopped bacon or pancetta
6 eggs
200 g natural yoghurt
2 tablespoons grated parmesan

1   Preheat oven to 220°C.
2   Line a tart shell or flan tin with pastry, prick base
    with a fork and refrigerate for 1 hour.
3   Heat oil and sauté silverbeet stems and onion with
    bacon or pancetta for a few minutes until bacon is
    crisp and vegetables are soft.
4   Add silverbeet leaves and fry for a few more minutes,
    then leave to cool.
5   To blind bake, line the chilled pastry with baking
    paper and fill with baking beans, rice or pastry
    weights. Bake in the oven for 8–10 minutes.

6 Remove baking paper and weights. Return to oven for a further 5–10 minutes or until light golden, then remove from oven and allow to cool.

7 In a mixing bowl, lightly whisk eggs and yoghurt together until well combined. When spinach mixture is cool, add to eggs and pour into blind-baked tart shell.

8 Bake the tart in a moderate oven for 20–30 minutes or until the top is golden and an inserted skewer comes out clean.

VEGETARIAN OPTION
Omit bacon.

THE COMFORT ZONE

I have never been one of those people who loses their appetite at times of distress or anxiety. There have certainly been times when I have been too exhausted or depressed to cook a decent meal, but lose the desire to eat? Never. In fact, I suspect that at these times I have turned to food—even more than usual—as a kind of nourishing constant.

After the deaths of her beloved husband and brother within months of each other, the great food writer MFK Fisher said this: 'One has to live, you know. You can't just die from grief or anything. You don't die. You might as well eat well, have a good glass of wine, a good tomato.'

Almost two years ago a friend's eleven-year-old daughter became suddenly, desperately ill with a condition that demanded emergency heart surgery and temporarily mystified her doctors. She eventually made a full recovery, thank goodness, but her parents endured several horrifying weeks by their girl's intensive-care bedside as she became sicker and sicker, suffering more and more complications.

At a loss as to how else to help, I left a few food parcels on their doorstep during those weeks, instinctively going for dishes high in fat, meat and carbohydrate: beef Bourguignon with mashed potato, chicken pies, lamb tagines with couscous. It was partly to do with the season—it was early winter—but I also instinctively chose foods associated with my own ideas of warmth and comfort. At first I wasn't even sure the parents would be able to eat at all, given the popular idea that people lose their appetite under great stress. But I soon learned, via the text messages through which word was spread, that food was exactly what they needed.

'We came home from the hospital each night absolutely ravenous,' Georgia told me later. Hot, hearty comfort food, in large servings, was exactly what they craved.

The idea of 'comfort food', and the widespread use of the term, only really emerged in the last decades of the twentieth century. And ever since, scientists and psychologists have been researching the notion of comfort food, what it is, and whether there is any truth in the idea that certain foods can provide a sense of consolation, emotional wellbeing or security.

Of course the definition of what kind of food makes a person 'feel better' is completely subjective, highly dependent on ethnicity and culture, age and even gender. But despite this, there does appear to be remarkable consistency in the kind of dishes that people, especially in Western cultures, describe as 'comfort food'. So much so that the *Oxford English Dictionary* now defines it as 'food that comforts or affords solace; hence any food (frequently with a high sugar or carbohydrate content) that is associated with childhood or with home cooking.'

But can food like this—mashed potato, say, or chicken noodle soup—truly affect our mood, alleviating sadness or distress? Well, it seems so. Many studies in both humans and animals show that food which is high in fat and either carbohydrates or sugar, or both, has a stress-reducing effect. This involves the release of chemicals in the brain—like serotonin and dopamine—that influence our moods and sense of reward.

One study by UK nutritionists showed that food rich in fat may reduce the amount of physical pain a person feels. In the study, eight men and eight women ate 'pancake meals' (which doesn't sound terribly delicious to me, but each to their own) before being subjected to a 'cold pressor test'—a cold-induced pain tolerance test in which your hand is immersed in iced water. The people who ate the high-fat pancake meals an hour and a half before the test were found to have a higher tolerance for pain than those who had eaten a low-fat version of the same food.

In another experiment, people were given breakfasts of the same calorie value but of different carbohydrate and fat content, and faced a series of cognitive tests before and after eating. They also had their moods rated before and after the meals. Although there was no clear difference in the cognitive performance, the group who ate the high-carb breakfast were in a better mood than those who'd eaten the low-carb meal.

There are all kinds of other scientific experiments measuring the way comfort foods promote feelings of wellbeing. It's been suggested that the 'palatability' of high-fat and high-sugar foods—foods that taste good—may improve mood by triggering the release of endorphins or 'endogenous opioids', those chemicals which activate what's called the pleasure pathway. Strange as it may seem, medical researchers at the University of New South Wales found that eating palatable food rich in fat and sugar can even alter the chemical composition of the brain, and reverse the effects of psychological trauma experienced early in life.

Brain structure and chemicals are only part of the picture. There is also a good deal of interest in the psychological component, with various theories suggesting that in times of stress we crave things that make us feel secure, that remind us of times we have felt safe (often related to childhood) and of people we love. A recent experiment published in the journal *Psychological Science* found that even thinking about comfort foods (in a writing test) made participants feel less lonely. And immediately after the September 11 attack on New York's World Trade Centre in 2001, restaurateurs across the United States apparently reported increased sales of dishes such as soup, mashed potatoes and macaroni cheese.

Of course, all these studies on comfort food are still going on, and ideas and theories about brain chemistry and food are still being tested. There are also opposing theories, especially one named the 'comfort food fallacy', in which studies showed that, contrary to what we believe, we more often choose to eat this kind of food not at times of upheaval but at times when we already feel at ease. And I notice that none of these studies take account of the mood-lowering effects of what presumably follows a lifetime of this kind of eating—heart disease and diabetes and arthritis, and probably rickets, scurvy and all the other dreary effects of a diet that might consist purely of mashed potato and macaroni cheese.

But enough of science. For curiosity's sake, I conducted my own completely unscientific survey of the kinds of dishes my friends, family and acquaintances describe as comfort foods. Unsurprisingly, high-fat, high-carb and softly textured dishes came up again and again as 'my favourite comfort food'.

Almost all the dishes listed by the sixty-odd respondents to my mini-survey were hot—only two people mentioned cold foods. One of these was the respondent's own homemade gluten-free biscuits and the other was cold custard. I think we can safely classify both of these as 'outliers'. Cold custard? Gluten-free? Comfort?

'Cheesy' foods came very high on the list, from my husband's instant answer of a toasted cheese sandwich to the very popular macaroni cheese, as well as 'cheesy dumplings', cauliflower cheese, and parmesan-smothered pasta.

Casseroles, soups and slow-cooked red meats were also big hitters: 'Pretty much anything from a crockpot,' said one, which summed up the school of thought that encompasses beef Stroganoff (which a Brazilian friend claims is a national dish in his native country!), lamb shanks, Irish stew, osso buco, and slow-cooked molasses beans.

One of the strongest trends was towards rather blandly flavoured and very softly textured foods, which appears to support the suggestion that we associate emotional security with foods from childhood. For these folks, comfort apparently means a return to 1950s England:

porridge was a huge favourite, as were other 'childish' foods such as poached and scrambled eggs, baked beans, lots and lots and lots of mashed potato, macaroni cheese, pikelets and rice pudding. On a similar theme, 'my mother's Yorkshire pudding' was mentioned surprisingly often.

Vegetarians may not have the slow-cooked meats in their comfort food armoury, but they too were proponents of the soft, wet, slop-and-stodge approach: macaroni cheese, pumpkin soup, porridge, and pasta with butter and cheese scored high on their lists. But they were often more culturally eclectic, reporting much higher preferences for dhal and other creamy lentil dishes than the meat-eaters, as well as vegetarian curries and lasagnes.

Which brings me to the non-Anglo comfort foods. Interestingly, these still tended to the soft, spoonable and carb-loaded variety: various lentil dhals, rice congee, Vietnamese pho, Japanese agadashi tofu, the Greek lemon and rice soup *avgolemono* and pad Thai noodles, for example, were mentioned often. An exception to this carb-loaded list was Brazilian *goiabada*—a sweet paste made from guavas, similar to the quince paste many of us eat with cheese. But given that *goiabada* in Brazil is most commonly eaten with Minas cheese, a combo known as 'Romeo and Juliet' for its perfection, I'm still allowing it as a comfort food under the cheesy foods heading.

Chicken soup in its various guises was, of course, a common favourite—from the revolting packet or canned chicken noodle soup of our childhoods to Chinese chicken and sweet corn soup, Lebanese chicken *yakhnet*, and of course the Jewish penicillin, chicken soup with matzo balls.

I have to say one dish particularly surprised me in its popularity as a comfort food. Australians, be proud: according to my entirely unrigorous survey, Vegemite toast is alive and well as a national comfort food. 'Vegie' toast was mentioned at least a dozen times, most often stipulated as desirable only in a white-bread and loads-of-butter combination. Perhaps the most ardent fan of this one was my sister, Bernadette, who said the first thing she had to eat immediately after giving birth to each of her three sons was 'hot toast made with thick white bread cut from a tank loaf with real butter and Vegemite and a hot cup of tea'.

All this has made me think about my own favourite comfort food. First, it absolutely must be hot—just as we were taught in first-aid class to cover a person suffering shock with a blanket, I think comfort food requires a sense of near-smothering warmth. It must also be able to be eaten from a bowl, one-handed, while lying on the couch—which leaves a hand free for either a wine glass or remote control. For this reason soup, while high on the list of comfort desirability (especially minestrone or chicken brodo), doesn't quite qualify for me; one slip of the spoon or tip of the bowl and the result could be a trip to the burns unit. So despite the heartbreak of excluding all my beloved tagines, chilli and basil Thai stir-fries and curries that came so close, I'm calling my number-one comfort food as a four-hour, high-tomato, high-fat, high-protein, high-carb and high-parmesan-quotient spag bol.

SPAGHETTI BOLOGNESE

*This makes a huge amount of Bolognese sauce. Keep it in
tubs in the freezer for those days when cooking is out of the
question, and comfort is required.*

Olive oil

500 g pork mince

1 kg beef mince

A little milk or cream

2 rashers bacon, chopped

1 onion, finely chopped

1 bunch thyme, leaves picked

½ teaspoon chilli flakes

1 stick celery, finely chopped

1 carrot, finely chopped

6 cloves garlic, finely chopped

2 × 400 g cans diced tomatoes

500 ml chicken stock

500 ml red wine

Salt and pepper

Dried spaghetti

Parmesan cheese, to serve

1   Heat olive oil over high heat. When hot, add pork
    and beef mince, in batches and cook, stirring, until
    liquid has evaporated and meat is well browned.

2   Add a spoonful or two of the milk or cream to the
    meat and continue to cook until liquid has gone.

3   Remove meat from pan and set aside. To the same
    pan add bacon, thyme, chilli and all vegetables except
    tomatoes. Cook on medium heat until soft, about
    10–15 minutes.

4   Add tomatoes, stock and wine and bring to the boil,
    stirring occasionally.

5   Reduce heat to a very low simmer and cook, covered,
    for 3–4 hours. Check liquid now and then, topping up
    with water if it begins to dry out.

6   In the last 30 minutes, raise the heat and reduce liquid
    to desired level, checking seasoning.

7   Cook spaghetti until al dente, drain and then return
    to the pasta pot with a few big spoonfuls of sauce,
    stirring to coat pasta.

8   Serve in wide shallow bowls with a big spoonful of
    sauce and grated parmesan.

POMMES BOULANGÈRE

Serves 4–6

*I thought I invented this, until I discovered it was a classic
French comfort dish.*

1 kg potatoes, peeled and sliced in 5 mm rounds
1 leek, finely sliced
3 cloves garlic, thinly sliced
3 cups chicken stock
½ cup thickened cream
Small sprig rosemary
Salt and pepper

1   Layer the potatoes, leek and garlic in a shallow, oven-
    proof glass dish.
2   Pour the stock and cream over the top, and push
    the rosemary sprig into the middle of the dish until
    hidden. The liquid should be just enough to come up
    to the top layer of potato—don't drown them.
3   Season (but be careful with the salt, depending on the
    saltiness of your stock, as it'll intensify as it reduces).
4   Cover with foil and bake in a moderate oven for about
    20 minutes.

5   Remove from oven and check whether the spuds are too dry—add more stock and press the potatoes down into the creamy liquid if needed.

6   Return to the oven without the foil and bake for around 1 hour, or until golden on top, occasionally pressing the spuds again if necessary.

7   Remove from the oven and rest for a few minutes before serving at the table.

DUCK RAGÙ WITH PORCINI

Serves 6

4 duck legs and thighs

4 tablespoons olive oil

1 onion

1 carrot, finely chopped

4 cloves garlic, chopped

1 stalk celery, chopped

1 bottle red wine

2 × 400 g cans tomatoes

1 cup chicken stock

2 bay leaves

2 sprigs thyme

1 sprig rosemary

Handful chopped fresh field or other mushrooms

30 g dried porcini, rehydrated and chopped

Salt and pepper

1   Remove as much fat and skin as possible from the
    duck legs and discard, then remove meat from the
    bones and chop into small pieces.

2   Heat oil and add onion, carrot, garlic, celery and some
    salt, and sauté until onion is translucent. Add the
    bones from the duck.

3   Add wine, tomatoes, stock and herbs and bring to the
    boil, then turn down to a simmer.

4   In a separate pan, heat some oil and add a pinch of
    salt, then sauté the duck meat until lightly browned
    and just cooked. Remove from pan and set aside.

5   In the same pan, fry the chopped fresh mushrooms
    until liquid has evaporated, then add these and the
    chopped porcini and liquid to the sauce. Stir, then
    simmer uncovered for around 30 minutes or until the
    sauce has reduced by half.

6   Remove the bones, add the duck meat and cook over
    low heat for another 20–30 minutes or until the meat
    is tender and the sauce is thick and rich. Add stock or
    water if at any stage it becomes too thick.

VEGETARIAN OPTION

A mushroom ragù without the duck is equally good. Omit
duck and replace chicken stock with vegetable stock or water.

SEE ALSO

Spinach dhal (see page 79)

Chicken and mushroom pie with green peppercorns
(see page 93)

Roast chicken (see page 111)

Florence Nightingale Soup (see page 180)

Cottage pie (see page 242)

THE MERCY MEAL

It seems strange to me now that I have no memory of what we ate after my mother's funeral. My siblings and I were all in our twenties or early thirties by then, after all, and reasonable cooks. Surely we must have prepared something to eat for the large gathering of people who would come back to our mother's house after the church service and the burial in the town where she lived and raised a family for more than thirty years.

But when I recall the day of her funeral, I don't think of food at all—I think of flowers. I remember how we spent the morning kneeling on the frosty grass in her garden, threading a large piece of gauzy white fabric with fresh flowers, for draping over the coffin once we got to the church. In the dreamlike surrealism that surrounds such a task, we had chosen the least offensively ugly coffin from a brochure. But almost as soon as we had done so, we knew we had to disguise it in some way—allowing our lively, dignified, nature-loving mother to be symbolised by that hideous varnished thing would have been like dressing her in a pinstriped power suit instead of what she did wear, which was the flowing skirt and top with the subtle ivy pattern that she had worn to our brother's wedding. (Oh, and bed socks—at the last second before the funeral people took her away, my sister said, 'I can't stand seeing her feet bare,' and leaped to cover our mother's feet in fluffy pink bed socks. It was exactly right, for it was chilly mid-July, and she had always hated cold feet.)

The blanket of flowers turned out to be exactly right, too. She had been a florist and was a keen gardener all her life, with a cottage garden full of tumbling annuals and perennials, herbs and vegetables. So the moment our mother's body was covered with a cloth of flowers was the moment the funeral began to belong to her, not the church or the funeral director or even to us.

I heard a beautiful term recently at the Orthodox Christian funeral of a friend's father—we were invited back to the Lebanese family's house for 'the mercy meal'. I couldn't go to that part of the ceremony (which I regretted for more than one reason—we later had a phone call from a friend who went, raving about the Lebanese spread on offer), but I was moved by the phrase itself, in a way I didn't really understand. I gather various cultures call the gathering after a funeral the mercy meal, rather than the word 'wake', which seems to be used most often among Australians of Anglo heritage.

I'm not sure why, but I've never really felt natural saying 'wake'—it conjures up such thoroughly Irish images of wood-panelled pubs and furious drinking and singing and raucousness, which hasn't really suited the temperaments of most people I've known who've died. Or maybe it's just the bluntness of the word itself. I much prefer the cadence and evocation of the 'mercy meal', although as a non-religious person I'm unsure of where the mercy might come from, and who exactly it should be for.

Perhaps one of the reasons I don't recall the food after my mother's funeral could be because we didn't prepare much of it—I have no doubt the close community in the town we grew up in brought platters of food for Mum's friends at the house afterwards.

I don't remember eating after my father's funeral ten years earlier, either. But I do recall the opening of many bottles of the wine he had spent years making with his best friend, Dave. During the ten years or so before he died, Dad and Dave had spent long companionable hours together making wine from all kinds of outlandish ingredients. For years the dark silence of night in our house was punctuated every few minutes by the gentle *blib-bloop* of the wine fermenting in the big demijohns in the kitchen.

Their wines, with intricate curlicued labels illustrated by our father—who had, in his one youthful, romantic year as a Trappist monk, taught himself the art of manuscript illumination—were made from all kinds of ingredients found to hand. Dad might have lived in Australia for the preceding three decades of his life, but his wines harked back to folkloric England: a dark red blackberry wine, the sauterne-like orange wine, dandelion wine, even one made of oak leaves and raisins. While the wines improved (and even, in one extremely proud moment, won a medal at the Canberra Wine Show), they shared one major characteristic: a terrifically high alcohol content.

As with my mother's funeral, I have no detailed memory of the hours of the gathering after Dad's. Possibly we were still all rather in shock, although we had known for some time his death was coming. But when I look back now at that day, I have one singular memory: standing on the veranda he had built, with a glass of his high-octane orange wine in my hand, gazing out across the streets of our town up to the windy, tussocky hills where he had taken us kite-flying in our childhoods. Wondering how life was supposed to go on.

I regret now that we weren't old enough to send off our father properly, in the way we could with our mother years later. But he had arranged much of the funeral service himself, and his friends took care of the rest. I remember only bits of the day—distantly, in a slow, glazed way. But I remember the wine.

A few months ago my friend Jane had the devastating duty of arranging a funeral for her adored cousin, killed in an accident just before Christmas. Noel lived in the small Tasmanian coastal town of Cygnet, and took his dinghy out several times a week to fish. After he died, people who had loved him began to gather in town from throughout the country, put up and fed by local friends. Food to feed the masses was prepared all over town, and they wanted the Tasmanian salmon Noel had caught and cooked for them so many times as part of the feast. But in the week leading up to his farewell, whenever Jane and her cousins took the net out, they came back empty-handed. Early on the morning of his funeral Jane and her brother rowed out to set the net one last time, beseeching the skies: 'Come on, Noel, we need the fish!'

Just before it was time to dress for the funeral, Jane and her cousins went out once more in the boat. As they neared one of Noel's favourite spots in Copper Alley Bay, she could see floats dipping—they had caught one! The three women leaned over the lip of the boat and began to heave in the net. Into the boat slithered six fat, shimmering salmon.

I love that story, with its biblical evocations—loaves and fishes, a plea to the skies, plenty granted where emptiness had been.

I wonder what the purpose is, the significance, of eating at a funeral. It cannot be to do with ordinary hunger, but it seems we have a deep need to eat together at this time, for food is involved in mourning ceremonies all over the world, and throughout history. Some cultures have special ceremonial funeral foods, like the *koliva*, the boiled wheat cake brought to funerals by Greeks, Serbs, Romanians, Bulgarians and other Eastern Europeans.

A friend recently hosted the wake of a reclusive neighbour who drowned on the beach across the road from both their houses. The funeral director told my friend there should be no fancy food (barbecued salmon certainly wasn't on the list). He told them plain sandwiches and cakes would be most suitable. The same week I heard of another funeral—for a mother who had died, too young, of cancer. She was a caterer; the cooking and sharing of food had been the central motif of her life. Her friends were asked to bring something special to eat and they were glad to do so, preparing, presenting and sharing with one another the platters heavy with bountiful, delicate food. It was the most apt and moving way for them to say goodbye: an expression of who she had been, the sharing of food was a communal letting-go.

One of the best funerals I've ever attended was that of my friend Pete's elderly father Neil. After their dad died, Pete and his brother sat together trying to figure out the most appropriate place to hold the funeral. Their dad had been a country man, a cropduster pilot, and an atheist. A church was out of the question, but so too seemed the sterile, oddly corporate non-denominational 'chapel' at the city crematorium. Pete said idly he wished they could just hold it in his house, and prop their dad up in the front room. His brother said, 'Well, why can't we?' And that is exactly what happened.

Their father's closed coffin lay in the front room, along with some photographs and other emblems of his life. It was a peaceful, lovely thing to stand alone in that room for a few minutes and offer a private goodbye. The rest of the house was given over to the small gathering of mourners for a cup of tea, a glass of wine, something small to eat, and remembrance. Not everyone was at ease with the intimacy of this arrangement: an elderly aunt of the family sidled up to me and asked what she was supposed to do—was there to be a priest, or a service? What would happen?

Not knowing what to say, I simply gestured towards the teapot and the table laden with sandwiches and sausage rolls, cakes and slices. And once she had a teacup in her hands, she was comforted. When, shortly afterwards, Pete and Nugget spoke briefly about their dad and then invited others to speak if they wished, the aunt began to say a few words, and then could not be stopped. Unrehearsed stories and memories poured out from her and other aunts and uncles, one tale prompting another as they spoke. It was the most natural, intimate ceremony of its kind I had ever seen: a man farewelled in a house he knew well, by people who loved him. Only at the very end of the day, when most people had gone, did the funeral car come to bear the coffin away for cremation.

Perhaps the food at a funeral serves as a physical ritual of familiarity: the pouring of tea, the passing around of plates might be the same kind of distraction that ambulance officers create when they ask bystanders to make cups of tea—providing occupation for the body until the mind can emerge from its blankness. Perhaps eating at such a time is a symbol of how the body must be cared for while the mind finds a way, somehow, to respond.

In her memoir *Feed the Hungry*, American novelist Nani Power writes, 'When people attend funerals, they eat desperately, almost in a rage against life.' But if what Power says is true, that people eat with gusto at funerals, might it not be from the opposite impulse—an unconscious surge of the life force, a rage not against life but against death? Maybe our need to eat together at a funeral is born of a fiercer, more primal instinct than we like to contemplate: survival. Perhaps it's a crucial step in drawing a line between the dead person and ourselves, between the past and the future, death and our life yet to be lived.

A platter of well-made sandwiches is the perfect food for a funeral, both practically and symbolically. It can be made ahead of time, cater for all tastes and appetites, and—in the literal breaking of bread—be a consolation shared.

CLASSIC MIXED RIBBON SANDWICHES

Choose different kinds of thick-sliced bread: wholemeal, rye, white or grain. Once sandwiches are assembled, use a sharp knife to remove crusts and cut each sandwich into three rectangles. Arrange the sandwiches on a plate, alternating different fillings, with the cut side up so guests can see which fillings are which. Take care not to make fillings too wet, and cover the platter tightly with plastic wrap until ready to eat.

CHICKEN

Chicken breast meat, poached or steamed, cooled and
    shredded
Celery, finely chopped
Capers, rinsed and well drained
Parsley, very finely chopped
Homemade mayonnaise, or whole egg or soya mayonnaise
Salt and pepper

1   Mix all ingredients, adjusting quantities until you have
    a fresh creamy mix with a hint of sharpness, neither
    too stiff nor too runny.

H AM

Good-quality seeded mustard

Butter

Smoked ham off the bone, torn

Emmental cheese, sliced

Salt and pepper

1   Spread mustard generously on one slice of the bread and butter on the other, then layer the ham and cheese and season.

S MOKED SALMON

Dill, finely chopped

Homemade mayonnaise, or whole egg or soya mayonnaise

Lemon

Salt and pepper

Smoked salmon

1   Combine dill and mayonnaise in a bowl with a squeeze of lemon juice until you have a spreadable herb mayonnaise that is not too runny. Season. Spread on bread before adding salmon.

Egg

Curry powder

Homemade mayonnaise, or whole egg or soya mayonnaise

Hardboiled eggs, peeled and finely chopped

Watercress leaves, picked

Cucumber, seeds removed, sliced

Lemon

Salt and pepper

1   Combine a teaspoon of curry powder with mayonnaise and chopped egg, adjusting to taste. Mix in watercress and cucumber and squeeze lemon over. Check seasoning before spreading over bread.

THE SOLACE OF SOUP

🍅

As a cook one has certain duties, I sometimes feel. And one of mine is to rescue the reputation of soup.

For a short while I thought the title of this book might include the word *soup*, which to me evokes the warmth and complexity and nourishment I wanted the book itself to symbolise. But it was wrong: as a title it sounded wan, sad, thin. It conjured invalidism, and produced the same kind of depressed, miserly feeling that causes my friend Vicki to set her jaw, fold her arms and declare that she *hates* soup.

I know what she means. There is something wrong with the way we Anglo Australians have experienced soup that took me years to recover from. Maybe it has something to do with the paucity, the hollowness and the lack of cadence in the word itself. *Soup*. Slop. Slump. Contrast this with *ribollito*, or *minestrone*. Or *harira, bisque, pho, bouillabaisse, tom yum, gazpacho*.

But the word itself can't bear all the blame for soup's bad reputation. I think one of the biggest obstacles is a textural one; I thought I disliked soup for many years, and when I thought about it, the texture of badly made soups was to blame. As I've said elsewhere, my mother was not exactly a passionate cook, but a competent one who took the nutrition of her family seriously. Our diet consisted almost entirely of unprocessed food; we ate fresh (often home-grown) vegetables, mostly brown bread, very little salt, sturdy cuts of meat, fruit grown in local orchards and other nutrient-dense stuff. There was no takeaway food beyond a *very* occasional parcel of hot chips from the fish and chip shop next to the Savoy Cinema (oh, the joy of this, and the triumph when it was you who got to nurse the scalding paper bundle on the car trip home, shifting frequently with the exquisite pain of your burning thighs).

But despite all this, there was one form of convenience food our mother wholeheartedly embraced: tins. Like *soup,* the word *tin* seems to have something of the Great Depression about it to my ears (we never said 'canned', which must have sounded far too American for my English parents), but tinned soup, tinned spaghetti, tinned baked beans and tinned peaches were my mother's saviours on the astonishingly rare days when cooking a two-course meal for seven people—this after the daily baking of some kind of cake or slice for afternoon tea—became too much effort.

She must have cooked real soups now and then, but I barely remember those; what we adored was tinned tomato soup, thickened with milk, eaten with fingers of hot buttered toast. If you mention 'tomato soup' to my husband, on the other hand, he visibly blanches—along with his siblings, he remains scarred by the tinned tomato soup their father 'made' every time their mother went to hospital to have a baby. Their dad's soup-to-milk ratio was rather out of whack, resulting in a tepid liquid of the palest pink. Ours, however, was a deep, rich (some might say unnaturally lurid) ochre colour. I can't remember really what was so delicious about it, except perhaps that it was so laden with salt that we found it irresistible. That, and the fact we were allowed to eat it in the living room while watching television, sitting picnic-style on a tablecloth on the floor.

I still feel rather fondly towards tinned tomato soup—a feeling which does not extend to the other tins which became more numerous in our house as we grew into teenagers expected to prepare our own weekend lunches and snacks. Unlike my older sister, who could cook, and made gorgeous pies and cheese soufflés and savoury tarts, I was lazy. Condensed Soup became a lunchtime staple, at least for me. I can't think of these cans now without a wash of nausea: Cream of Chicken, Cream of Mushroom, Chicken and Corn. Or the other kind, the ones called things like Farmhouse Ladle or Thick'n'Chunky. All of these made the same horrible sucking sound as they glooped out of the tin, a wobbling tower of rude-smelling sludge, still holding the shape even of the ridges of the can, until water or milk was added and, like the Leaning Tower of Pisa, it gradually sank into defeated disintegration. The colour was ghastly—either a ghostly grey-white or an orange-studded brown—and the texture was always the same. Now I suppose that the uniformly sludgy texture (even the separate vegetable lumps were just smaller, separate units of the same gloop) was the result of combining emulsifiers, modified maize starch, potato starch, soy extract, 'egg products', 'milk products' and 'natural flavours'. But back then, it seemed this was simply the texture of *soup*. I obviously didn't loathe it then, as I seemed to eat so much of it, but in memory it has curdled into vileness. (In my mother's defence, she must sometimes have made soup from fresh vegetables, because childhood memory also recalls another soup horror: *barley*. It may even have been our vociferous hatred of barley that led her to throw up her hands and embrace the can. I have recently grown to love pearl barley, but this was different stuff, with a nasty hairy quality. I wonder now if I have imagined this, but the memory is so strong I feel there must be something in it. There was something reminiscent of insect antennae about the hairy bits of barley. (Which reminds me of a friend who told me recently she quite likes quinoa, but 'I can't eat it with my glasses on. I can't look at the little tails.')

After the Cream of Mushroom years, I avoided soup of all kinds for at least a decade. I didn't even like *people* who liked it—they seemed, like soup itself, somehow droopy and spiritless, lacking in backbone or substance. I suppose the reputation of soup as diet food may have added to my aversion; who could claim to love something that was all about denial and hunger, guilt and restraint? This period of my life also coincided with the ubiquity of pumpkin soup on every café and share-house menu. Sickly sweet, bright orange and often thinned to stretch the quantity, it was as miserly as the others except it seemed compulsory to love it, which made the fact of it even worse, gob of cold sour cream or no. Only very recently could I return to pumpkin soup, and that's because it was made by a Sri Lankan friend whose version contained almost as much ginger and chilli and other spice as pumpkin.

But my main problem with soup, perhaps, though I was never conscious of it, was the fact that soup *is* so good, so exactly right, when one is sick or exhausted. So I think now that my aversion to soup was a good and natural one, sensibly shared by most young people. Youth is not the time one *should* want nourishment and healing—far better, in your twenties, to be wrecking one's body with excesses of every kind. And maybe it's not until one actually truly needs the comfort of a good soup that its appeal can be properly, bodily, understood.

It was a visit from my Aunty Pat that revealed to me exactly how luxurious soup could be. Pat is an excellent cook, who makes the kind of good British food made famous by people like Delia Smith. Proximity to Europe, I suspect, gave my aunt a flair for cooking that my mother, who moved to Australia at nineteen, always lacked. To this day Pat's food is simple, modest, yet always richly flavoured and beautifully textured. She stayed with me in Sydney during the dreadful early part of our mother's surgery and radiotherapy for a fatal brain tumour, a time now tinged with such horror I can remember it only as a blur of hospital visits, our mother's shaven head and her bouts of vomiting. When I think of how it must have been for Pat, crammed into a tiny flat not only with my partner and me, but sharing a bedroom with two of my sisters for week upon week of terrified misery, I am ashamed of how little I thought of supporting her. But I was still in my selfish twenties; in that shocked and frightened time I simply slotted my aunt into our mother's role, expecting her to care for us rather than the other way around.

I had a job not far from home at the time, and when they were not at the hospital I would come home and meet Pat and my sisters for lunch. I remember the first day our aunt presented us with deep bowls of velvety vegetable soup, accompanied by hunks of crusty fresh bread. This soup was like nothing I had ever eaten. It tasted, looked, smelled and felt sumptuous in the mouth: earthy, as richly coloured as mahogany, spiced with complex layers of heat and flavour, it warmed the chest and the spirit in some deep, nourishing way. It was exactly what we needed.

As I wiped my bowl clean with the bread, I asked Pat how she had made it. Where had the ingredients come from?

'Oh,' she said, 'just bits and bobs,' gesturing in the direction of the lower part of the fridge. The *fridge*? I was appalled: the 'crisper'—which as comedian Billy Crystal has pointed out should more accurately be referred to as the 'rotter'—surely had held only a couple of limp carrots, half a dried-out onion and a yellowing celery stalk. *This* could not have come from *that*. But it had, with the addition of a little stock, and olive oil and garlic and tomatoes, and a judicious amount of whizzing in the food processor to create the velvety texture and meld the flavours so perfectly.

So that was my conversion to soup. As is so often the case when a disliked food is prepared by a good cook, the transformation seemed miraculous. Still, it took another decade or so until I became a fully fledged soup-maker myself. Working from home has had something to do with this—for convenience, very little beats simply ladling into a bowl some rich vegetable soup (into which has gone bacon and homemade chicken stock and lentils or chickpeas or beans and a parmesan rind), topped with a thread of walnut oil or a dollop of pesto. And I must be growing very old, because these days part of the motivating factor for making soup is the thrill of saving food from waste. Of course I like to think of it as part of an environmental crusade (and it is—food rotting in landfill gives off methane, a greenhouse gas twenty-five times more potent than carbon pollution created by car exhaust, and each Australian throws about 136 kilos of food per year into the garbage), but what I really love is rescuing all the 'bits and bobs' from their fate as compost. I love creating something rich and aesthetically pleasing from something seemingly so lacking, so poor: a lump of leek, a single sprouting potato, a drooping celery stick and a drying knob of ginger. And a soup recipe is such an adaptable creature; any vegetable you have to hand can be added, from half a capsicum to a wheel of eggplant to a can of lentils. The only essentials in my soups are onion and garlic—from there, the possibilities are endless.

Chilled soups are another wonder I have only recently discovered. A couple of summers ago, on the hottest day for sixty years, some friends and I flopped about a beach house trying desperately to cool ourselves by wandering in and out of the shower all day, then draping ourselves before an array of electric fans, all on full throttle. Oddly presciently—we'd had no idea the temperature would climb to *48 degrees Celsius*—very early that morning I had made a soup of lettuce, leeks, green peas and mint, and bunged it into the freezer. At nine o'clock that evening, when the temperature had dropped to a crisp 36 degrees and we sweltered on the deck in our swimming costumes and wet sarongs, we ate the icy green soup, each bowl topped with three chilled prawns and a dollop of yoghurt. It seemed a gift from the gods of cool.

Chilled leek, pea and cucumber soup with prawns

Serves 4

A cooling summer lunch or light supper. Unlike many cucumber soups, this one contains no cream but is quite filling.

Olive oil
2 leeks, finely chopped
8 Lebanese cucumbers, peeled, seeded and chopped
½ bunch dill, chopped
1 litre chicken stock
1 cup frozen green peas
½ 400 g can cannellini beans, drained and rinsed
Salt and pepper
12 cooked prawns, peeled (tails left on if desired)
1 tablespoon chopped mint

1   Fry leeks gently in olive oil till softened.
2   Add cucumber and dill and cook for a few minutes.
3   Add chicken stock, cover and simmer for about
    20 minutes or until vegetables are very soft.

4   Remove from heat and add frozen peas—they will
    quickly soften and help cool the soup.

5   Add cannellini beans.

6   Purée soup with a stick blender or in a food processor
    until smooth or desired consistency—it can be
    rustically thick.

7   Check seasoning—depending on the saltiness of the
    stock, salt may not be required.

8   Cool and then chill in refrigerator for several hours.
    (The soup can be served at room temperature, but is
    best served quite cold.)

9   To serve, ladle soup into bowls, top with three prawns
    per bowl and scatter chopped mint over the dish.

VARIATION

Omit the cannellini beans and use 2 baby cos lettuce,
chopped, in place of cucumber.

VEGETARIAN OPTION

Skip the prawns and use vegetable stock in place
of chicken.

CAULIFLOWER SOUP

Serves 6

1 tablespoon butter

Olive oil

2 small onions, diced

1 head cauliflower, broken into small florets

1 litre chicken or vegetable stock

4 sprigs thyme

2 bay leaves

Salt and pepper

1   Heat the butter with a good glug of olive oil. When the butter starts to foam, add the onions and sauté over low heat for a few minutes until soft.

2   Turn up the heat, add cauliflower and sauté for 10–15 minutes, turning regularly so it has a chance to turn golden all over.

3   Add the stock and herbs, then turn down the heat and simmer until cauliflower is very soft.

4   When cauliflower is falling apart, purée the soup with a stick blender or in batches in a food processor until thick and creamy.

5   Season with salt and pepper.

PHARMACY IN A BOWL

Serves 8

Feed this to anyone who has a cold—they will feel better instantly.

Olive oil
5 cloves garlic, finely chopped
1 brown onion, finely chopped
2 small red chillies, finely chopped
1 stick celery, finely chopped
1 leek, finely chopped
¼ white cabbage, finely chopped
1 red capsicum, roughly chopped
3 carrots, roughly chopped
3 litres chicken or vegetable stock
1 head broccoli, roughly chopped
1 × 400 g can tomatoes
1 cup Puy lentils
Salt and pepper
Grated parmesan, to serve

1   Sauté the garlic, onion, chilli, celery, leek, cabbage, capsicum and carrots in batches in the oil until well browned.

2   Put the chicken stock in a big pot on the stove and
    bring to the boil, tossing in all the sautéed ingredients.

3   Add broccoli and tomatoes, and simmer until all
    vegetables are tender.

4   Reserving stock, remove vegetables with a slotted
    spoon and purée in a food processor or blender until
    smooth (or roughly blended, depending on how rustic
    you like your texture).

5   Return puréed vegetables to stock and add lentils.
    Simmer for 15–20 minutes or until lentils are tender
    (more if you want them falling apart). Season well
    with salt and pepper.

6   Serve with a sprinkle of parmesan.

BOUILLABAISSE

Serves 6

12 large prawns

Olive oil

1 leek, finely chopped

1 small fennel bulb, roughly chopped

3 cloves garlic, finely chopped

1 stick celery, chopped

Splosh of white wine

1 litre chicken stock

1 × 400 g can diced tomatoes

3 strips orange peel

A few threads saffron

Pinch dried chilli flakes

½ kg black mussels, cleaned

½ kg perch or other firm white fish, cut into 4 cm chunks

1 blue swimmer crab, cleaned and quartered

1 tablespoon chopped fresh dill

Salt and pepper

1   Peel and devein prawns, leaving tails on and setting aside the shells and heads.

2   In a heavy-bottomed saucepan, heat oil and toss in shells and heads, stirring over high heat until pink, then add leek, fennel, garlic and celery and stir until softened and starting to caramelise.

3   Deglaze with the wine, then add the stock.

4   Remove as much of the prawn shells and heads as you can using tongs—but don't panic if a shred of shell remains; what's a crunchy bit of crustacean between friends?

5   Add tomatoes, orange peel, saffron and chilli flakes. Bring to the boil and simmer for around 30 minutes.

6   A few minutes before you're ready to eat, add the fish and cleaned seafood and turn the heat to low or even off.

7   Check for seasoning, and serve in big bowls with a drizzle of olive oil.

HEARTY BEAN STEW

Serves 6

2 cloves garlic, chopped

1 onion, chopped

1 carrot, chopped

1 stick celery, chopped

Stems from ½ bunch silverbeet, roughly chopped

Olive oil

1 teaspoon fennel seeds

1 × 400 g can tomatoes

2 bay leaves

1 cup chicken stock

1 × 400 g can borlotti beans, drained and rinsed

Leaves from ½ bunch silverbeet, roughly chopped

1 large zucchini, sliced into rounds

2 slices pancetta

½ chorizo sausage, sliced into rounds

Crusty bread and garlic cloves, for rubbing

1   Sauté the garlic, onion, carrot, celery and silverbeet stems in oil until tender.

2   Add the fennel seeds, tomatoes, bay leaves, stock and borlotti beans, simmer for 20 minutes.

3   Add the silverbeet leaves and zucchini, cook for a few minutes and then turn off the heat.

4   In a separate pan, fry pancetta and chorizo until
     brown and crisp.

5   Return the soup to heat, then divide among bowls,
     each topped with a crisp of pancetta and a few
     chorizo slices. Serve with garlic-rubbed crusty bread.

VEGETARIAN OPTION

Use vegetable stock in place of chicken, and replace
pancetta and chorizo with a chopped chipotle chilli soaked
for a few minutes in boiling water.

Spicy mussel bisque

Adapted from Jared Ingersoll's crab bisque recipe
Serves 4

1 teaspoon each cumin, caraway and coriander seeds
½ teaspoon fenugreek seeds
150 ml vegetable oil
1½ large red capsicums, seeded and chopped
4 cloves garlic, squashed
2 ripe tomatoes, chopped
1 stick celery, roughly chopped (it may be worth peeling this
     first if you can be bothered)
1 medium fennel bulb, roughly chopped
1 red onion, chopped
⅓ cup soft brown sugar

Pinch chilli flakes

Salt and pepper

1.5 kg black (or 'blue') mussels

1 large glass white wine

600 ml chicken stock (I use homemade—if you use packaged, omit seasoning the soup until the last minute, if
necessary)

½ bunch coriander, leaves and stems separated

Crusty bread, to serve

Optional: 2 tablespoons harissa—I love Yalla harissa and
keep a pot of it in the freezer for digging into to add
extra kick to all kinds of dishes. If you don't want or
can't find this, you could perhaps double the spice mix
and chilli at the beginning for some extra kick.

1   Preheat oven to 180°C.

2   Toast the spices in a dry frying pan until fragrant,
then grind in mortar and pestle or spice grinder.

3   Heat a deep roasting tin in the oven or on the stove
top and, when hot, add the oil and all the vegetables
except coriander leaves.

4   Sprinkle the spices over the vegetables with the sugar,
chilli flakes and seasoning, and mix well. Roast in a
moderate oven for about 1 hour.

5   Meanwhile, scrub and de-beard the mussels, then
place in a covered pan with a big glass of white wine
and simmer over a medium heat for about 10 minutes,

or until the mussels are opened. Remove them from the pan to cool, reserving the cooking liquid. When the shells are cool enough to handle, remove the meat from the shells and set aside.

6 When the vegetables are soft, smell good and are a little coloured, remove from oven. Transfer the vegetables and the mussel meat into the large bowl of a food processor and purée until smooth—or keep it coarse if you prefer a more rustic texture.

7 In a sizable pot add the stock to the mussel cooking liquid, then add the purée and simmer gently for about 15 minutes.

8 Add the chopped coriander leaves and harissa if using, stir to combine, and serve with crusty bread.

DO I DARE TO EAT A PEACH?

To me this has always been the most poignant phrase of J. Alfred Prufrock's love song, with its yearning for a lost sensuality, and the devastating idea that the mere fact of age might exclude one from even the simplest of earthly pleasures.

I confess that a loss of delight in food, more than many other aspects of physical decline, is one of the things that frightens me most about ageing. And it seems that this is almost inevitable. Ask around and you'll hear some colourful tales of dietary foibles among the elderly. My friend Peter's father, for example, an ex-farmer who lived in a city flat for the last few years of his life, subsisted surprisingly well for a long time on oranges, frozen chicken nuggets and Cadbury's Dairy Milk Chocolate from the corner shop. Another friend reported that her mother-in-law, an excellent cook and lifelong abhorrer of junk food, fell in love with McDonald's cheeseburgers when she reached her eighties. She and her husband ate them five times a week. And yet another told me that during the last few months of her grandmother's life, the only food the lady wanted

224

was hot chips. She would eat just four or five of them, very slowly, with a glass of brandy.

Of course if you're lucky enough to reach eighty or ninety or a hundred you should eat whatever the hell you please—even if, it pains me to say, your former passion for fresh figs and labneh, or braised lentils with herbs and pancetta, is replaced by a much stronger love affair with powdered Deb potato, two-minute noodles and Diet Coke. That said, I desperately hope this doesn't happen to me.

Thankfully, individual experiences differ as much in old age as in any other part of life, so I cross my fingers. But the fact remains that many people who have adored food, cooking and eating all their lives seem to lose their zest for it when they grow old.

One of the reasons for this is sheer physiology. This should come as no surprise—children have many food aversions and textural preferences as their bodies grow and transform, for example, and pregnant women's food cravings are legendary. So the body's changes in old age represent just another stage of the way we respond to food. As one reaches one's seventies and eighties, the various senses inevitably begin to dull. But while eyeglasses and hearing aids can help to alleviate failing sight and hearing, there's no cure for the naturally diminishing senses of smell and taste—the primary drivers of pleasure in food. The tastes for sugar and salt are the first to fade, apparently, which might account for your grandmother's emptying your salt shaker whenever she visits, or your father-in-law adding those extra three or five spoonfuls of sugar to his coffee.

The dulling of the palate is partly to do with the fact that the tastebuds themselves disappear as we age. We're born with around

10,000 tastebuds, but we begin to lose them after about the age of forty to fifty for women and fifty to sixty for men, although there's debate over exactly how much loss is age-related. One source says that a person could lose between 20 and 60 per cent of their tastebuds after the age of sixty!

But one's sense of taste is not just affected by natural bodily changes. The fact that we tend to take more medications as we age may also be a factor—antibiotics, chemotherapy drugs and some arthritis medications can alter the sense of taste, and if you are unlucky enough to have Alzheimer's or Parkinson's disease, the attendant neurological changes can affect taste too.

Of course, pleasure in eating does not only have to do with flavour and our ability to detect it. Even if the spirit is willing—drooling, even!—for that extra-spicy curry or butter-laden chocolate cake, the flesh may be weak. Indigestion, heartburn, gall-bladder or other gastrointestinal issues can make new enemies of old favourite dishes—yet another dreary fact that many of us begin to experience even in middle age.

Mouth changes might take place too. It's often assumed that we produce less saliva as we age, with about a quarter of older people finding they have a dry mouth much of the time, but dental experts say there's no clear link between age and dry mouth. Regardless of the cause, though, a dry mouth can make some foods unpleasant to eat. Teeth are another issue—J. Alfred's fear of the peach could potentially have as much to do with the discomfort of fruit fibres stuck in the dentures as his existential anxiety. If one did have teeth problems, together with the fading sense of taste, I can see the appeal of a squishy, salty, textureless chicken nugget.

But all this focus on the body and its various betrayals can be a way of medicalising what for many of us is a complex mixture of far deeper issues: being tired, being lonely, simply being *sad* as your family disperses, or your partner dies, or your friends move away or succumb to illness.

Several older people have told me they used to love cooking but have lost enthusiasm for it now they live alone. Particularly for women who may have spent decades cooking nightly dinners for large families, making the adjustment to single-portion servings can be difficult. I understand this, because although I've always cooked a proper dinner for myself, even in the years I lived alone, there's a certain logic in not wanting to mess up two saucepans, a frying pan and serving dishes—which you then have to wash up—all for the sake of dinner eaten solo. It's not hard to see why lots of older people—especially if their appetite has also waned, as it often does—settle for a piece of toast and a cup of tea instead. For older men the picture can be even more complicated, as many men of my parents' generation never learned to boil an egg, let alone cook a nourishing meal. I wonder if this might be part of the reason so many men quickly follow suit when their partners die. Each of the friends who related the examples of junk-food-loving older folk thought the convenience of these foods was as much a part of their appeal as the salty-sweet factor.

And while there are options for home-delivered meals, I sympathise with people who want nothing to do with them. I do not look forward to the day I'm told I'm too infirm or old to fend for myself with food; I suspect I will be one of those who respond less than graciously to the idea of outside 'help'. Pete's father, for example—he of the oranges and chicken nuggets—used to flush the council-provided dinners down the toilet as quickly as they were delivered. I don't blame him. A phobia of institutional, mass-produced food is one of the reasons my food-loving friends and I are constructing an increasingly serious fantasy about an elderly gourmands' commune for our last years. Those hot-food transport bags and ugly melamine-lidded dishes are simply too depressing to contemplate.

I like to think, however, that there's a world of difference between a meal delivered as an invalids' health service and a home-delivered dish as an act of love from friends or family. I have sometimes cooked meals in the home of an older friend, and at the same time added a few tubs of food to his freezer. This can be tricky, because it's crucial this sort of cooking doesn't feel to the recipient—or the cook, for that matter—like an act of charity. This will largely depend on personalities, but there are ways of preserving a person's dignity. Eating a meal together is perhaps the best. The conviviality of a shared table—perhaps with one or two of your Aunt Janet's friends as well as yourself—is likely to remove any charitable overtones, and you can make sure the cleaning up is done before you leave, so nobody is left with a mountain of washing-up.

A visit for dinner is also a good opportunity to sling a couple of Tupperware containers into the freezer. I have found that making the portions about half the size I would for someone my own age is also a good idea. Most older people eat nowhere near the amount they did when younger, and I've seen an older friend instantly lose her appetite if a large plate of food is set before her. The same friend, served a much smaller portion, will often happily go back for seconds. It seems that even just the *idea* of too much food can be quite a turn-off. This is where our habit of serving food from communal bowls on the table works well; self-serving means nobody gets more than they want, but a second helping is de rigueur.

I've also taken to freezing soups and casseroles in half-sized portions and giving them to another friend (still frozen) to take home if he visits us or we drop by his place. This transfer must take place speedily, breezily and with discretion—put in the car or bag at the last moment, for example. If visiting, we make sure any container is labelled and just leave it in the fridge. (All the usual disclaimers apply about safe transport and storage of food, keeping food chilled and so on. Food poisoning is dreadful for anyone, but for a person of advanced years and some frailty, it can be fatal.)

One of the best stories I've heard about food and growing old is that told to me once when I had made devils on horseback—the salty, sticky snack of a prune wrapped in bacon, then barbecued, that was all the rage at dinner parties in the 1970s. I love devils on horseback, not only for their rich flavour and textures, but for the fact they remind me of childhood, of the specialness and excitement of my parents' progressive dinner parties. And I suspect I'm not the only one who loves them as much for their retro glow as their taste.

When my friend Virginia's grandfather had a stroke, he became very sad and almost completely lost his appetite.

'This lasted until, for some reason, I came up with the idea of taking him some devils on horseback,' Virginia says. 'Perhaps I'd made some for a party and he initially got the leftovers. He *devoured* them. Mine had cheddar cheese in the middle. I was nicking off from work in the middle of the day to rush home, grill the devils and then courier them out to his rehab hospital twice a week, and he was much cheered.'

One of the reasons I love this story is that it challenged my expectations and suppositions about cooking for older people. It's clear that while many of us will turn to milder flavours and even quite bland food as we grow old, the tastes of others will remain as adventurous, and their favourite foods as full of flavour and evocative of memory and pleasure as they ever were.

DEVILS ON HORSEBACK

Makes 12

In honour of Virginia's grandfather, and in the hope that age may not inevitably weary our tastebuds.

100 ml orange juice

2 anchovies, finely chopped

5 sprigs thyme, leaves picked

12 pitted prunes

12 blanched almonds

12 slices of pancetta (or the equivalent strips of bacon)

1   Mix orange juice, chopped anchovies and thyme in a bowl.

2   Add prunes to the juice and leave them to plump for 10 minutes or so.

3   Push an almond into the centre of each prune and wrap it in a slice of pancetta—if using bacon, only use as much as needed to wrap once around the prune—then secure with a toothpick.

4   Barbecue (or place under a hot grill) for a few minutes, until the pancetta is sizzling and cooked but not burned.

THE PRIVATE WINTER: COOKING DURING CHEMOTHERAPY

'Chemotherapy is a little like a private winter,' writes Brenda Walker in *Reading By Moonlight: How Books Saved a Life*. 'It brings its own weather, independent of the clouds or sunshine outside the hospital . . . it's an icy climate, chemotherapy, and it's difficult to carry a living story out of that grey place, to set it down in light and warmth and hope it might hold together.'

Over the years I have watched several people close to me endure the bitterness of the season Walker describes so movingly. Every time, I have been awed by their fortitude and dignity as each of them endured the long months of this often brutal treatment. The mental strength required for such suspension of disbelief—acceptance that what feels like poisoning may be your only chance of survival—is immense.

It is easy to glamorise other people's suffering, and words like 'bravery' and 'courage' have been rendered meaningless by sappy overuse in the realm of cancer treatment. It's not as though chemotherapy is ever really a choice, and I doubt anyone feels brave.

Each person I observed found their own way to persevere mentally while the body endured what it must. I don't wish to dwell on those times, but I do want to share what I have learned about one's capacity to help.

As a well-meaning onlooker, I think it is very important to first be clear about one's motives, and to ensure one's own feelings do not override the needs of the person one wishes to help. If I am honest, I look back at my responses to the life-threatening crises of some friends with not a little shame. As a young woman prone to dramatisation and over-identification with the suffering of others, I was slow to learn how crucial, and how much more respectful than dramatic gestures, are small offers of practical help on which one can definitely deliver. Decades ago, a close friend's baby was diagnosed with an unusual and terrifying brain tumour. I lived near the hospital and, in a panic of sympathetic despair, began making a meal and taking it to the parents at the hospital every day. I did this for a few weeks, as the treatment went on and on and the distress and terror grew worse. I set my work aside, and spent each day shopping and cooking whatever I thought might please them. The day came, of course, when I just couldn't face going to the hospital and seeing that tiny wasted body, and their despair, one more time. I sent a message to say I couldn't come. I was far too ashamed to admit I couldn't deal with it anymore; I can't remember what reason I gave. Nor do I know what they thought—possibly they were too distressed even to notice—but I have always regretted that I didn't behave more calmly and rationally. Slave to my own emotions, I bombarded them with love and hysteria, then abruptly abandoned them. They all survived—the baby is now a perfectly healthy young man—and I never felt an iota of judgement from that couple. But I still regret how badly I handled it.

I think this must be one of the most hurtful responses to a long-running crisis of the kind that chemotherapy involves. Everybody wants to help at first, but so few of us manage to stay for the long haul. If there is one piece of clear advice I can give to those wanting to help a friend in a crisis, it's this: make small, realistic offers of practical help, think about the long term, and *follow through*.

Cooking is both a practical act and an expression of love, and can be—when appropriate—a useful contribution. But cancer therapy affects people so differently in terms of their appetite and desire for food that there are no firm rules on what or how to cook. We tend to talk about 'chemo' as if it's a drug, when in each case the therapy is a different cocktail of drugs targeted at the individual, varying even within the same forms of cancer. In fact, it may be more practical to think about this kind of support in terms of cooking for carers and family members rather than the sick person. While some appear to make it through aggressive chemo and radiotherapy regimens with their weight and appetite unchanged, others experience side effects so nasty that eating anything at all is difficult. I have asked as many people as I can about their experiences of cancer treatment, and their answers, together with my own experience, have yielded a few salient lessons about supporting someone through a time like this.

The first point is: *ask*. Most people want to help, and spend a long time worrying about how to do it. The simplest way is to ask what you can do—but be specific. Email and text messages are a godsend because your friend can respond when they wish and is not obliged to speak to you if they're not up to it. A common error is to say, 'Let me know if there's anything I can do.' This will not be heard as a serious offer of practical help.

Unless you are very close to the person (and often even then), they won't ask for your help. For one thing, just getting through the day requires enormous effort; thinking of jobs to allocate to different friends will not be high on their priority list. It's up to you to make concrete, specific offers that sound low-key and easy for you to do. 'I'm going to the supermarket—I'd love to do your grocery shopping while I'm there.' Or 'I have a quiche I want to drop off to you—can I leave it on your doorstep tomorrow morning?' (See page 239 in this chapter for food safety tips.)

While everyone is different, my strong hunch is that it's best to err on the side of keeping in touch rather than leaving the person alone, but only if your contact can be unintrusive. Dropping off a tub of chicken soup unannounced on your way to work may be acceptable—but going inside for a cup of tea is not. Of course, one knows one's own friends and family best; perhaps all that's required is to pay attention to what's *not* said as well as what is.

Widen the circle   If you can't cook, or feel it's too intrusive to keep dropping by, some metropolitan areas have services you can pay to deliver good, nutritious, home-cooked food. One woman I know rallied a group of friends to pitch in the cash to pay for one gourmet meal a week for six months from a service like this, delivered to the young family of a friend with cancer. For this family the arm's length approach was perfect—they were not required to be bright and grateful, or even speak to the deliveryman if they didn't feel like it, and weren't obliged to respond to anything but the initial offer, which they found very moving.

Lower your expectations about your food being enjoyed   If, like me, you are deeply attached to the idea of food as love and nourishment—and if your sense of self is tightly bound up with having your food appreciated—then cooking for someone having chemotherapy will seriously undermine that idea. Louise, a zealous cook, told me the hardest thing about cooking for a family member having cancer treatment was abandoning the idea that her food would result in pleasure, comfort, or even basic physical nourishment. 'I usually cook for and experience food with great joy,' she says. 'It's a big part of my life. So that was the toughest part, and the bit I'd probably pass on as advice—don't expect much.'

Foods that are tolerable one day might be unbearable the next, for example. Or food the person specially asks for, or even craves, might turn out to revolt them when it's presented. Louise spent a couple of weeks trying to find the exact brand of strawberry milk that her family member had enjoyed in hospital. Almost as soon as she found it, that same milk became intolerable.

If the person is having trouble eating anything at all, either because of lack of appetite or because of nausea or other stomach troubles, dietitians recommend they try several small meals a day instead of three normal-sized ones—something to remember if you are packaging portions for delivery or particularly for freezing. It's a good idea to buy small containers and fill them with very small portions, even if they look silly to you. Your friend can always eat more if they're hungry, but even just the appearance of a big portion of food will put some people off eating completely.

Be prepared to experiment and change tack all the time Side effects vary so much between people—and even over the course of one person's treatment—that foods which alleviate some problems might exacerbate others. For example, metallic or bitter tastes might be helped by lemony or spicy marinades, but those same marinades can worsen the pain of mouth ulcers or a sore throat. So try to keep in touch with what's going on side-effect-wise. Some common side effects of chemotherapy are an inability to tolerate spices or chilli, rough textures, acidity or strong smells and flavours (fish, for example). Food (and wine) often develops a metallic or bitter taste, and many people having cancer therapy also develop painful mouth and throat sores and ulcers, making acidic or sharp-tasting foods completely impossible. If in doubt, stick to mildly flavoured foods with soft textures. 'Imagine you are feeding a baby' is something cancer services often advise—even to the point of puréeing mild-tasting vegetables and stewed, non-acidic fruits.

One piece of advice I read is to never serve a favourite food on or around chemo days—the mental association of that dish with nausea or other unpleasant reactions could last forever. In fact, timing in general can be quite important. My friend Lu, who had about a year's worth of hard-core chemo and radiotherapy, the former made worse by an excruciatingly painful problem with her veins, recalls: 'For me, the process worked like this. You would have a chemo session and feel dreadful that day but otherwise not feel too bad for a few days. By a week later your white blood cell count has dropped and you are pretty miserable. Then the cell count recovers and you are starting to feel actually quite well again, relatively, when—whaddayouknow—it's three weeks later and time for the next blast. Then, if you have six chemos, each time gets worse.'

Emergency stays in hospital because of the effects of chemotherapy are common. Lu's experience, reiterated by other friends with similar experiences, showed that the best time to receive food, visits and so on was in the week *before* each chemo session, when she was at her strongest.

Often if a person can't eat, they can drink—although mouth problems can make this difficult. Cold, soft foods and drinks can help, as can drinking through a straw to bypass painful areas of the mouth (and tastebuds if taste changes make food unpalatable). Homemade ice blocks like the ones we had as children can help in this situation; I am thinking of my sister's delicious elderflower cordial here—sweet, subtle and not too acidic. Protein shakes, while they may look depressing to a healthy person, can be helpful for someone in this situation.

The upside of cooking for someone having cancer treatment is that you can forget the usual notions of a healthy diet—all the high-fibre, low-fat advice goes out the window at a time like this, when the general aim of the game is to maintain weight rather than lose it. So, providing your friend's digestive system can tolerate it, creamy soups and pasta sauces, lots of eggs, cakes and biscuits—high-calorie, high-protein, high-carbohydrate foods—are desirable now. Providing as many vitamins and minerals as you can is good, but often the more important issue is simply keeping up the calories when the person finds they can eat. That said, many people cannot stomach fatty, highly spiced, meaty or fried foods.

Don't forget small things   Your friend may not be able to look at the quiche or the casserole you've made, but the packet of Fruit Tingles, jubes or jelly snakes, or the dried apricots or cashew nuts or ginger biscuits you include in your delivery might be exactly what they need. A friend in hospital with leukaemia years ago could eat hardly anything, but devoured the tamari almonds I bought on a whim from a health food shop. Other things that might be worth trying are hummus and pita bread, cheese and biscuits, or edamame beans (you can buy them frozen from Asian grocery stores—just cook them as you would frozen peas), which are all high in protein as well as other nutrients.

Be fanatical about food safety   You will already know that people having cancer treatment are exceptionally vulnerable to infection. This means that in preparing meals you need to be absolutely scrupulous about food hygiene: wash your hands obsessively before and during food preparation; keep all food preparation areas clean with hot soapy water; scrub fruit and vegetables clean; keep raw meats away from other foods with separate utensils, chopping boards and so on; make sure meats are cooked adequately; cool foods quickly and refrigerate immediately (as soon as steam stops rising); thaw any frozen foods in the refrigerator and make sure any transported food is kept cold in an insulated bag with accompanying ice bricks. It goes without saying that you can't visit your friend if you have a cold or any other minor infection. I would add that even if *you* don't have a cold but you share a house with someone who does, it would be courteous to stay away from your immunocompromised friend—even the fear of catching a cold is enough to cause someone in this situation enormous stress.

Remember the carers   There will be many times through a course of cancer therapy where your friend is not up to any kind of communication—they will just want to be left alone. But this doesn't necessarily mean their family or carers should be abandoned. One of the greatest stresses on a sick person is the idea that they are causing their partner or family to suffer, and your support of the carers is just as important—and, often, much more practically effective. If there is anything the sick person's partner or kids especially like to eat, add that to any care package for the person herself.

Flowers might be beautiful, but for an exhausted family they can be more of a hindrance than a help. 'A lot of people sent us flowers,' says Lisa, who had breast cancer. 'Which was lovely, but not so helpful. We didn't have room for them—especially as our side tables were now devoted to medical paraphernalia, and in the end it was just more work for my partner to manage.'

More important to her, she said, was that her husband was kept fed and well. She was especially grateful to a friend who occasionally took her husband out somewhere nice for lunch. And when she herself was too sick to eat, and he was worn out from the hospital trips and changing her bed linen twice a day because of her night sweats, at least her husband was nourished by the food their friends brought them.

COTTAGE PIE

Serves 8

It's easy to get lots of nutrients into this classic comfort food, but you may need to vary the vegetables according to the person's ability to tolerate them. This recipe makes two large trays or several smaller ones—using disposable aluminium foil trays means nobody has to keep track of containers or dishes. This also freezes easily.

Olive oil
2 kg beef mince
1 fennel bulb, finely chopped
1 leek, finely chopped
2 carrots, finely chopped
2 sticks celery, finely chopped
½ red capsicum, finely chopped
3 cloves garlic, finely chopped
6 mushrooms, chopped
2 handfuls French-style lentils or Puy lentils
¼ cup Worcestershire sauce
¼ cup light soy sauce
1 tablespoon tomato paste
1 tablespoon honey

Salt and pepper

1 cup frozen peas

8 potatoes, peeled

50 g butter

½ cup milk or cream

Oil or melted butter

1   Take a large heavy-based frying pan or casserole and brown the meat thoroughly in a little oil over high heat. Remove meat from pan and set aside.

2   Add a little more oil if necessary and sauté fennel, leek, carrot, celery, capsicum and garlic until soft.

3   Add mushrooms, lentils, Worcestershire and soy sauces, tomato paste and honey and stir to combine.

4   Return the meat to the pan, add 2 cups water, season, cover and cook for around 40 minutes or until flavours have developed. Remove lid near the end of cooking, add peas and reduce sauce to desired consistency—thick and soft, but not stiff.

5   Meanwhile, place potatoes in a saucepan of cold water. Bring to the boil and cook, covered, for about 20 minutes or until tender. Drain well, return to pan, add butter and mash until smooth, then add milk and stir to combine. Season.

6   Fill trays with the meat sauce, then top with mashed potato, smoothing it out to the edges of the pan.

7   Preheat grill to high heat, and drizzle a little oil or melted butter over the mashed potato. Place cottage pie under grill for 10–15 minutes or until topping is nicely golden.

TAMARI ALMONDS

400 g raw almonds
3 tablespoons tamari sauce
1 tablespoon vegetable oil
Salt

1   Mix all ingredients well and leave for about an hour, stirring now and then to make sure the almonds are well coated.

2   Line an oven tray with baking paper and spread almonds out, then roast in a moderate oven for about 15 minutes, removing the tray every 5 minutes to check and turn the nuts.

3   Leave to cool—they grow crunchier as they cool and dry.

4   When completely cooled, store in an airtight container.

A PARCEL IN THE POST

The writers Sylvia Townsend Warner and William Maxwell corresponded by post for forty years, from before World War II until Sylvia's death in the late 1970s. The collection of their letters, *The Element of Lavishness*, is one of my favourite books.

One of the pleasures of the collection for me is following the contents of the parcels they sent back and forth between New York and England during those four decades. Books and articles, of course, but other things too: seaweed emulsion (Sylvia to William), onion skin paper (William to Sylvia), or the packet of sweet pea seeds she smuggled to him between the pages of a book. The latter was doomed, because customs officers unwrapped the parcel, removed the seeds, then 'replaced the beautiful wrapping paper and string—as if nothing had happened!' (I must have been influenced by the pressing of things between pages as I read the letters, because when I opened the book just now to reread, a cicada's single perfect wing fell out onto my desk).

The letters themselves, of course, are the superior gifts, revealing a friendship of exquisite intelligence; tender, sharp and witty. But other than words, some of the most lavish gifts are of food—mostly from William to Sylvia during the food shortages in England following the war. It is delightful to trace their contents through the letters. In 1947, when he was her editor at the *New Yorker*, William offers to send her canned tomatoes. In March 1951, Sylvia reports that 'a magnificent ham arrived' at the same time as a flood—she and her girlfriend Valentine moved to a friend's house for the night, where Sylvia kept the ham in her bedroom. A few pages on, in June 1952, she promises to use well 'that noble parcel of butter' William sent. As late as June 1954, he was still sending food; Sylvia thanks him for the arrival of 'a package of the most delicious and gluttonous beef', which she began eating in bed that very day, after falling down the stairs.

The letters echo the excitement I still feel when even the most modest package arrives in the post. To me, a parcel containing food is the most cheering of all. I have been delighted in recent years to receive jars of homemade marmalade, lemon butter and chutney, packages of shortbread and cheese biscuits, my sister's renowned mince pies—even a slightly soggy envelope of garlic chive seedlings—in the letterbox. In turn, I have sent all kinds of food through the post. The easy things are those in jars, cellophane bags or boxes: roasted tomatoes from the garden preserved in oil, preserved lemon, tomato chutney, spiced nuts. The trickier—and therefore more thrilling—things are perishable: chocolate brownies and parmesan biscuits at the safer end, but also pomegranate honey, chilled vacuum-packed cured salmon, and cooked and frozen meatballs.

The sense of excitement comes, I think, from the risk and the humble romance of the gesture, its sheer impracticality. Will the container hold? Will the contents break or spill? Will the recipient be home to receive it, and if not, might it be left somewhere a passing dog can sniff it out and tear the package open? Or, as with Sylvia's sweet pea seeds, will the postal service confiscate the parcel entirely in the name of public safety?

The writer Gay Bilson famously posts her sorrel soup all over the country. In *Plenty*, she tells of a friend phoning to ask for the soup recipe. Instead:

> I went for surprise and posted her a containerful of soup:
> aluminium for insulation, bubble-wrap, sticky tape and
> a prayer for a safe overnight journey. There was the odd
> stomach-wrenching turn when I thought about what other
> people's mail would look like if things went wrong, but
> once again sorrel soup proved its travelling credentials.

I think there are two main impulses at work in the desire to send food in the post. The first is Bilson's kind: the urge to delight and surprise. And because the posting of food—especially something as potentially disastrous as soup—happens so infrequently, the surprise and delight must surely be greater. The second is the impulse to comfort someone in distress or crisis. When William offered to send canned tomatoes to Sylvia, his hope was that it might 'brighten the corner where you are'. Such are those food gifts sent to alleviate homesickness. When my sister was at boarding school, now and then my father would send her and her best friend Annie each one of his stupendous pork pies. The rare fact of his cooking at all made the parcel all the more special. And—I found out after my mother's death—for a couple of years after she had stayed with us for short periods as a troubled foster child, a girl called Tracey at the same boarding school would now and then receive a cake tin full of my mother's Anzac biscuits.

How miserable the first waves of migrants to Australia must have been without their familiar foods. How dreadful for it to first dawn on a Greek or Turk or Italian or Arab immigrant, for example, that there was no olive oil to cook with here, that in its place they were expected to use dripping or butter or, worse, margarine. It is almost impossible to comprehend that within my own lifetime there was a period when olive oil was only sold in small quantities in pharmacies as medicine for constipation! How many people in the 1950s and 60s received the extravagant bounty of a tin full of olive oil from home? Or when chillies were unheard of, how precious that first envelope of seeds, how tenderly guarded the seedling and carefully harvested the fruit to save its seeds for another crop.

War must be the most dreadful form of dislocation and home-sickness of all, and perhaps the most poignant food parcels have been those sent not only for emotional comfort, but as the basic means of survival. During World War II, the Red Cross sent weekly food parcels to allied soldiers held in prisoner-of-war camps across Europe. A typical parcel contained tea, cocoa, a bar of chocolate and all sorts of tinned goods, including pudding, meat roll, 'processed cheese', sardines or herrings, jam, sugar, vegetables, biscuits and 'dried eggs', along with soap and cigarettes.

The Maxwell–Townsend Warner food gifts, interestingly, began around the time the actual term 'care package' arose—immediately after the war had ended. In 1945, the newly-formed CARE (the Cooperative for American Remittances to Europe) began sending food relief to Europe, where large numbers of people were now at risk of starvation. For ten dollars, ordinary Americans were able to buy a CARE package—an unused US Army food parcel—to send to friends or relatives in Europe, and these were guaranteed to arrive within four months. After the surplus military packages ran out, the organisation made up civilian ones. Each CARE package contained one pound of beef in broth, one pound of steak and kidneys, eight ounces each of various pickled and preserved meats, two pounds of margarine, a pound each of lard, jam, honey, raisins and chocolate, eight ounces of egg powder, and two pounds each of sugar, whole milk powder and coffee. A couple of name changes later, the humanitarian organisation continues under the name CARE, which as a global organisation now stands for the Cooperative for Assistance and Relief Everywhere.

Care packages are still sent today by ordinary people to soldiers at war. In the US, soldiers can request something called (rather nauseatingly) a HeroBox, a custom-filled package of things the individual soldier has requested. Australia's soldier care-package system is doubtless less practical, but rather more touching. Anyone can send a parcel—which will be delivered free of charge by Australia Post if you buy the right box and it's under two kilograms—addressed to 'An Australian Soldier' in Afghanistan, East Timor or the Solomons, care of the Department of Defence. There are websites dedicated to lists of good things to send. These include breakfast cereals, ring-pull tuna cans or sachets, lollies, microwave popcorn, microwave rice (which I learn you can buy at 'reject shops' for two dollars), and sachets of mustard and tomato sauce from McDonald's. Homemade food is not allowed unless addressed directly to a named individual soldier. I suppose it is reasonable to send things the troops actually want, rather than indulging the passions and vanities of oddball home cooks around the nation, but it does seem a little sad to think Our Diggers will never be allowed the surprise pleasure of pomegranate honey or chocolate brownies or spiced nuts or chutney—or even Gay Bilson's sorrel soup.

After this, it seems clearer than ever that sending a parcel of perishable food through the postal system is truly a gesture of folly and romance. Which is exactly what makes it so desirable.

My friend Astrid lived for a while in Scotland, to pursue a brilliant business idea. But living in a country without family or close friends made Christmas difficult. She would normally be on an Australian beach with her huge extended family, but in Scotland she spent two Christmases alone, freezing and miserable. But one year she received a parcel from her sister and small nieces. 'I unwrapped a large black Vittoria coffee tin with a busted latch and blue kingfishers printed on the outside,' she recalls. Inside the tin was a small hand-painted card, saying: 'Made by Annabel, Luisa and Suzie with much love and under not-very-hygienic conditions'.

Under the card was an assortment of shortbread stars and triangles and emus with little silver balls pressed into them. Nothing else could have brought her greater comfort.

Covering less distance but even more adventurous were the parcels of fresh blue swimmer crabs sent by my friend Vicki's grandfather in Perth to his daughter and her family living in a little town in the Wheatbelt where, as Vicki puts it, 'the only thing interrupting the horizon on the way out of town was the silver snake of CY O'Connor's pipeline heading to Kalgoorlie.' Vicki's granddad would catch the critters in his crab pots in the Swan River, wrap them in ice, newspaper and brown paper, drive them to Perth railway station and put them on the train to Cunderdin. The family, alerted by telephone, would hurry to meet the train as it arrived—at midnight. Crab meat was a family obsession, it seems, for the same grandfather later could not bear to let Vicki's mother return home to Melbourne on the plane unless her hand luggage was stuffed with frozen blue swimmers.

I love the poetry of these things, and the timelessness of the solace brought by familiar foods in strange places. I like to imagine the citizens of ancient civilisations sending care packages to one another. A Persian mother, perhaps, pushing a little woven bag of lentils or some precious threads of saffron into her courier son's saddle bags alongside the papyrus scrolls, to take with him on a long journey. And travelling food is not limited to journeys on earth. Just as Soviet astronauts of the 1970s were given borscht and caviar to take with them into space, the ancient pharaohs took figs, bread, grapes and pomegranates—even a watermelon—into their tombs and from there, the afterlife.

POSTING FOOD: PRACTICALITIES

Posting perishables is best, I have found, when one can be certain the recipient will take the same foolhardy delight in the contents of the package that you have taken in sending it. If your recipient is the more cautious type, it is advisable to employ extreme packaging, and even perhaps include a note of reassurance about food safety and temperatures. According to food-safety authorities, perishable food (meat, dairy, seafood, cooked vegetables or fruits, cooked rice or pasta, fresh pasta, food containing eggs, vegetables or herbs in oil, etc.) can be reasonably deemed safe to eat if its temperature is outside the 'danger zone': 5 to 60 degrees Celsius. The Food Safety Information Council of Australia says foods held inside this danger zone for more than four hours should be thrown out; foods held in the danger zone between two and four hours should be used immediately; and foods in the danger zone for less than two hours can be refrigerated, or should be used immediately. If the food has not reached the danger zone at all—if it is still frozen, for example, or ice crystals are still visible—it is safe to refrigerate and eat as normal.

Australia Post advises that perishable foodstuffs may travel by post if the sender can: ensure that in the normal course of carriage they will arrive in time to be usable; pack the foodstuffs in receptacles that do not allow the smell of the contents to escape; in the International Post, pack the foodstuffs in rodent-proof receptacles (I confess I have never considered rodent-proofing!). My own tips for posting very perishable foods include using overnight Express Post, making sure the thing is frozen solid and very well sealed in an air- and watertight container, using as much insulating material as you can (soft insulation freezer bags of the type sold by butchers are good, as are polystyrene boxes), and soft or hard ice packs if necessary.

TOMATO CHUTNEY

1 kg ripe tomatoes (I use Romas but any will do), halved

350 g onions, roughly chopped

90 g raisins

180 g light brown sugar

1 birdseye chilli, with seeds, halved

1 teaspoon salt

2 teaspoons yellow mustard seeds

250 ml white wine vinegar

150 ml olive oil

1   Combine all ingredients except the oil in a pot, bring to the boil, then simmer for around an hour, stirring occasionally. If it looks too runny, turn up the heat and reduce until it becomes jammier. Add the oil, stir thoroughly and turn off the heat.

2   Meanwhile, sterilise your jars—I pour boiling water into the jars and over the lids and let sit for a few minutes, then drain and put them into a warm oven to dry (unless the lids are plastic, obviously) for another few minutes. Pour the hot chutney into hot jars, screw the lids on tightly and invert. Leave for 10–20 minutes, after which the lids should have gone slightly concave, making a good vacuum seal.

3   To post, make sure the lid is well sealed and secure
     well with bubble wrap and tape.

GRAVLAX

There are recipes galore for cured salmon, or gravlax.
A single fillet is easier to fit in the fridge than a whole side of
salmon—and when cured and vacuum-packed, it can even be
sent, well chilled, in the post!

1 thick salmon fillet, skin on (about 400 g)
1 tablespoon coarse salt
1 tablespoon ground pepper
1 tablespoon caster sugar
¼ cup vodka
1 bunch dill, chopped
3 juniper berries, crushed with the flat blade of a knife

1   Mix all ingredients except the salmon until well combined,
     then smother the salmon fillet with the mixture.
2   Place salmon in a flat-bottomed glass dish, skin-side
     down. Cover with cling wrap, then place weights on
     the fillet.
3   Refrigerate for 12–24 hours, then turn the fillet over
     and repeat on the other side.
4   Remove fish from dish, brush off excess mixture and
     pat dry.

5   To serve, slice the salmon very thinly (like smoked salmon) and eat on rye bread with a little crème fraîche, lime zest and capers.

6   To post it, leave the fillet whole, package well in plastic or vacuum seal, and insulate well with ice.

UNDER THE LIGHTHOUSE:
BEACH-HOLIDAY COOKING

🍎

One summer we holidayed with friends beneath a lighthouse on the coast of New South Wales. It was the head keeper's sprawling stone house, and we spent the days reading, dozing on the wide, encircling veranda or picking our way down the bush path to the long white sandy beach to swim. We stood on the lawn peering through binoculars at the schools of leaping dolphins or pods of whales moving through the turquoise water. Every now and then we would turn on the television to watch the drama of the Toowoomba floods unfold. From our idyll, those images of houses torn from their stumps and cars upended were even more shocking than they would otherwise have been.

Every night after dinner we would climb the hundred and fifty stone stairs to the lighthouse, each night amazed again by the dazzling majesty of it: the great bicycle-wheel spokes of light slowly crisscrossing and turning, washing the sea and the headland in silver light.

Perhaps it was the lighthouse which gave that particular holiday such a feeling of blessedness. The word holiday comes, of course, from 'holy day'; it has its origins in pilgrimage and worship. This seems perfectly apt—for Australians, that's just what the beach holiday is, a secular pilgrimage to the edge of the land, the worship of the wave. It is my absolute favourite kind of holiday: flopping down for a week in a house near the ocean with a group of easygoing, funny people who are happy to let the days slide in and out, like the tide, in a lazy, sandy drift. A tangled wetsuit on the clothesline, prawns in the fridge, sand in the hallway.

The winter holiday is a more subdued experience. I rarely take holidays in winter, but if I do, it's for the purpose of being still. In winter one travels inward, buries oneself in layers, hunkers down. Food is slow-cooked, doors and windows closed, the body seems to draw into itself for hibernation. For me, winter holidays are about introspection, consolidation, the quiet mind.

But a summer holiday is about outwardness, and casting off: clothes, fishing lines, expectation, inhibition. When I think of our holidays in summer the view is always *outward*, to water. Borders dissolve: doors and windows stay open, legs flop over hammock edges, bathers are worn out of water and in, and the living—sleeping, eating, bathing, cooking, arguing, reading, laughing—takes place as much outside the house as in it. Despite all the dozing and lazing, there is something very *physical* about the beach holiday. Skin is everywhere; being slapped and slathered with sunscreen, or getting sunburned, or even (gasp—the illicit childhood thrill of it) *peeling*. Feeling the needling sting of shower water on your sunburned skin, or yanking aside your swimming costume at shoulder or bum cheek to measure just how much forbidden tan you've developed—these gestures must be universal, yet they feel powerfully Antipodean to me. And why is the simple, bodily tiredness that comes from sun and swimming in the ocean so pleasurable?

The body is defiantly in evidence during a summer holiday, as much as it is hidden during the winter one. I think that with this uncovering, this embrace of the physical, comes something unusually tender and human. It's difficult to be self-protective, after all, when you're wearing what might as well be your underwear, sucking the juices from a prawn head while seated in a puddle of sea water. On the beach holiday one literally strips oneself bare. And if one is lucky, this exposure can bring with it an openness and trust, a declaration that *this is me*, a state of self-acceptance from which one might ordinarily shrink.

Then, of course, there's the food. For our friends, cooking and eating is absolutely central to the pleasure of the beach holiday. It is surely pure fantasy that food made at these times is better than at others, but there is something especially good about the grazing, shifting, tidal nature of this way of being, of the way meals waft and move and transform. Dishes are always shared and leftovers seem to last forever, shape-shifting between one meal and another and another until they're gone. The braised Iranian eggplant my friend Caro made during our lighthouse week, for example, morphed from the main dish at dinner to a side salad at next day's lunch to a spoonful of condiment on that evening's barbecued fish.

The communality of cooking on this kind of holiday is essential to the pleasure of the whole experience. For no matter what plans may have been made for divisions of labour, or responsibility for this or that meal, there is an inevitable overlap and convergence, which grows as the days pass and everyone relaxes. Unlike cooking at home, the creation of food on this type of holiday is serendipitous, adaptive, impromptu. There is a natural, cyclic rhythm of coming together and separating, and seeing, in a sense, what the tide brings in. Someone might walk in the door with an unexpected fish (invariably provided by the local seafood shop rather than the fishing rods we bring with us), or someone draws out from the back of the fridge a forgotten rockmelon that must be eaten now or wasted. Or you'd planned on pesto but left behind the pine nuts, or the local shop doesn't have basil, or there's no stick blender/mortar and pestle/lemon juicer in the house. So you substitute, abandon one plan and come up with another, combine ideas, and generally make do. It's liberating, this freedom from expectation, and there's a kind of lazy amusement in the challenge to one's resourcefulness. No colander? A tea towel will do. Out of couscous? Use rice instead. Nobody cares that the serving dishes are cracked plastic mixing bowls or the salad servers are a spatula and a wooden spoon. Someone returns from an op shop with a *Time Life Spanish Food* book, hauls an ancient electric frypan from the darkness of the cupboard beneath the sink, and suddenly tonight's seafood barbecue is replaced by a potluck paella.

I would like to think of myself as a light traveller, the sort of person who throws a sarong, a book and a sun hat into a bag, leaps into the car and hits the highway. Unfortunately the truth is I am the opposite kind—the one who brings a woollen scarf to the beach just in case the weather turns nasty, and half a library of hardbacks in case I get sick of the book I'm reading. I am trying to move in a minimalist direction, however, and my personal beach-holiday luggage is slowly shrinking to a single overnight bag. And I do mostly leave kitchen equipment behind, if only for the fun of improvising. Ingredients, though, are another matter—I seem unable to travel to an empty house even for a weekend without packing sea salt, balsamic vinegar, a zip-lock bag of fresh herbs, a head of garlic and some good bacon. I also never leave home without our best knife.

What does this say about me, I wonder? Probably that I am nowhere near as adaptable a person as I would like to think. The idea of going without salt or good salad dressing for a weekend, let alone a week, sets off a small but definite alarm deep inside me. Clearly, a more flexible person wouldn't give a damn. But maybe that kind of person cares less than I do for pleasure, or for the—to me—crucial detail that elevates a fine experience into a sublime one. Life is short, I want to say to that person (I see her as a no-nonsense Head Girl type, shaking her head at me in pity, or disapproval). It will all soon be *over*, I want to tell her. If all that's required is a little ballast of salt and garlic and leaves, why ever not make each meal as perfect as I can?

The pleasure of a meal is fleeting, of course. But might there not also be a more lasting one, in what is brought home—the images, tastes, sensations that live on in memory after the time has long passed? As everyone knows, one of the most potent qualities of the sense of taste is its capacity for transporting one from the present into the sharpest memory. And so it is that whenever I eat a thick wet slice of ripe tomato with a shred of basil leaf, I return to New Year's Eve in the little fibro house on the saltwater Lake Macquarie, when we swam in phosphorescence at midnight. Chilled pea and lettuce soup takes me to the hottest night of the century, when we slept on mattresses on the deck at Hardys Bay. Pippies from the beach—and a mouthful of sand—make me remember a surprise long weekend at Culburra, just as smoked trout and citrus couscous will forever summon camping at Esperance and the bluest water I have ever seen. A tumbler of Americano cocktail with a fat orange segment jammed into the glass takes me to Puglia and the Adriatic Sea—and Caro's mother Judith's fish cakes will always bring back to me the summer week under the lighthouse.

Each of these memories is as strongly connected to the people I shared them with as the place or the food. And if I travel with too many ingredients as a kind of nervous tic, they'll not be wasted—I can always take them home again. For some of the deepest culinary pleasure happens, I know now, in the space of happenstance and discovery, in the passing of technique or recipe or ingredient from one end of the kitchen bench to the other. In this way I have discovered that fish cakes can be just as good (and much easier) baked rather than fried, that pippies really need soaking for much longer than you think, that fresh oysters will last two or three weeks in a bucket in the shade if covered with a cool wet sack, and that I love Campari.

Perhaps the ideal beach holiday involves a replication of these things in us, too. If we bring our most essential selves and leave the protective layers behind, we might find that this abandonment to the moment, this opening out to possibility and to each other, is what deepens us, enriches us. Perhaps travel to the edge of the land can also mean a journey outward from ourselves—casting off inwardness, leaving old parts behind and finding new ways of being, new selves to take home again.

JANE'S CITRUS COUSCOUS
Serves 6

This is especially good served with the best holiday food—a moist, flaked smoked trout—and a huge dollop of soya mayonnaise on the side.

2 cups orange juice (about 8 oranges; best if freshly
    squeezed so you can use the pulp too)
1 knob butter
Salt and pepper
2 cups couscous
3 or 4 zucchinis, sliced on the diagonal
Olive oil
½ bunch shallots, sliced
1 teaspoon cumin
½ cup currants
½ cup pine nuts, lightly toasted
1 bunch mint, finely chopped
1 bunch coriander, finely chopped
Lemon juice to taste (about ½ a lemon's worth is good)

1   Bring orange juice to boil in a small saucepan with
    butter, salt and pepper. Turn off the heat and stir in

couscous until well combined. Leave for at least half
an hour.

2   Sauté zucchini slices in olive oil until well browned
and soft.

3   In a large salad bowl combine all remaining ingredients, and season well. Add the cooled zucchini to the
mix.

4   Take the saucepan and gently comb and scrape the
couscous with a fork until the grains separate—this
takes a while and it's important to be patient, otherwise you end up with big lumps. Empty the loose
grains into the salad bowl as you go. Often the last
thin layer has to be discarded.

5   Stir other ingredients loosely through the couscous
until well combined, then check seasoning.

QUINOA SALAD

Inspired by Caro and Ottolenghi

200 g quinoa
50 g wild rice
1 onion, peeled and sliced
3 tablespoons olive oil, plus a little extra for frying
Handful of barberries or dried cranberries or currants or any
    dried fruit
Zest and juice of 1 orange

1 teaspoon lemon juice

1 garlic clove, finely chopped

2 spring onions, thinly sliced

1 bunch coriander or basil or parsley, or a mix of these with
some dill

Large handful of pistachio nuts

Salt and pepper

1   Preheat oven to 170°C.

2   Bring to the boil two saucepans filled with salted
water, and simmer the quinoa and rice separately:
the first for 13 minutes, the second for up to 40,
depending on how nutty and firm you like the
texture.

3   Drain both and spread out flat to cool more quickly.

4   While the grains are cooking, fry the onion in a little
olive oil until dark golden brown. Allow to cool.

5   Soak the dried fruit in orange juice and zest in a bowl
with all other ingredients except nuts.

6   Dry-roast the pistachios in the oven for up to
6 minutes or just until the colour changes. Check
halfway through, because they can burn in an instant.
The flavour is vile if they are even slightly overdone,
and you'll have to chuck them out.

7   Mix the cooked grains with all the other ingredients
and season generously, adding a little swizzle of oil if
it's too dry. Serve at room temperature.

PUMPKIN, PINE NUT AND FETA SALAD

Serves 6

If it's well roasted and soft, I think pumpkin skin is lusciously bittersweet, and helps the pumpkin hold its shape. But if you really don't like it, remove the skin before serving.

500 g pumpkin, skin on, cut into large chunks

Olive oil

2 tablespoons pine nuts

1 bunch rocket

Balsamic vinegar

Salt and pepper

3 tablespoons marinated feta cubes

1   Roast the pumpkin pieces in a slosh of olive oil in a moderate oven, until soft and caramelised.

2   While the pumpkin is cooking, dry-roast the pine nuts on a separate tray in the oven for 5 minutes or until golden.

3   Remove both trays from the oven and cool.

4   Wash, dry and dress the rocket leaves with a dressing of 1 part balsamic vinegar to 3 parts olive oil. Add salt and pepper.

5   Arrange the leaves on a large plate and add the pumpkin, pine nuts and feta cubes—gently mix the salad so the pumpkin receives a coating of dressing without falling apart.

CORN FRITTERS
Serves 4

3 cobs corn
4–5 tablespoons rice flour
1 tablespoon yoghurt
1 handful each finely chopped basil, parsley and chives
2 eggs
½ teaspoon chilli flakes
Salt and pepper
Oil

1   Shuck the corn by standing the cob on its end and running a knife sharply down the side.
2   Mix everything except the oil in a bowl, adjusting the flour if it gets too watery (it does look unnervingly runny, but that doesn't really matter in the end).
3   Throw two-thirds of the mix in a food processor and pulse a couple of times to get a rough blend, then return to the bowl.

4   Heat some oil in a non-stick pan over medium-high
     heat and cook the fritters in batches. Depending on
     the amount of oil you use and the runniness of your
     mix, the texture tends more towards the pikelet than
     fritter, but either is delicious. Drain on kitchen paper
     before serving.

SALMON NIÇOISE SALAD

Serves 2

1 piece cooked salmon, broken into bite-sized pieces
5 kalamata olives
5 anchovies, roughly chopped
1 hardboiled egg, quartered
1 tomato quartered
Lettuce leaves
A couple of teaspoons of vino cotto (or balsamic and oil
    dressing)
A handful of cooked green beans, halved
Salt and pepper

1   Combine all ingredients and toss gently in the vino
     cotto or dressing.

TOMATO & BASIL

3 of the ripest, fattest tomatoes you can find
1 cup basil leaves, chiffoniered (cut into very fine strips)
Salt and pepper

1   Slice the tomatoes thickly and layer them on a plate.
    Scatter over the basil, season, and leave for at least 20
    minutes before serving.

JUDITH'S TUNA POLPETTE
Serves 6

These are good hot or cold, and freeze extremely well.

250 g ricotta
250 g tuna in oil, well drained
2–3 tablespoons grated parmesan
1 egg
Herbs, chopped (dill is especially good)
Salt and pepper
4 tablespoons fresh breadcrumbs—just enough to bind
    mixture so it is neither too dry nor too moist (or use
    almond meal for a gluten-free option)
Optional: capers, pine nuts, finely chopped semi-dried
    tomatoes, lemon zest

1   Preheat oven to 180°C.

2   Mix all ingredients, adding breadcrumbs or almond meal last, then refrigerate for a couple of hours to firm.

3   Line an oiled tray with baking paper.

4   Form mixture into small fish cakes or balls and bake in a moderate oven for 15 minutes each side, or until golden.

5   Serve with herby yoghurt (see page 276) or a spoonful of mayonnaise, herbs and lemon wedges.

ROASTED CARROT AND MINT SALAD
Serves 4–6

At least 1 kg carrots
Olive oil
1 bunch mint, finely chopped
Good balsamic vinegar
Salt and pepper

1   Preheat oven to 200°C.

2   Slice carrots into rounds about 1 cm thick.

3   Lay carrots in a single layer in a roasting pan (use 2 pans if necessary), and splash generously with oil until the carrot slices are well coated but there is not too much excess oil.

4   Roast in a hot oven for up to an hour, turning once or twice, until carrots are well caramelised. Remove from pan and set aside to cool.

5   Once the carrot has cooled, stir through the chopped mint, salt and pepper, and add balsamic vinegar a tablespoon at a time (about 2 tablespoons per kilo of carrots) until you have a sweet, sharp flavour.

6   Season well and serve.

COCKTAIL: THE AMERICANO

1 part Campari
1 part sweet vermouth
Soda water
1 wedge orange
Ice

1   Fill a chilled glass with ice cubes and the orange wedge. Add Campari and vermouth, and top up with a little soda water. To make this a Negroni, add 1 part gin to the mix.

SEE ALSO
Freshly shucked oysters (see page 144)

LISTS OF FIVE THINGS

FIVE FIDDLY THINGS I CAN'T BE BOTHERED TO DO

It was Shirley Conran who said, 'Life's too short to stuff a mushroom.' I have never stuffed a mushroom, but here are the tasks I baulk at for the same reason.

Peeling vegetables

I almost never peel vegetables, unless it's potatoes for roasting, but even then I mostly don't bother and just cut them into chunks. My mother's words about the most nutrition in vegetables being in or just under the skin still ring in my ears, and my obedience to her coincides nicely with my innate bone idleness. With a very few exceptions—celery for making Marcella Hazan's celery gratinée, for example—I urge everyone to scrub, not peel.

Skinning and de-seeding tomatoes

Very occasionally, if the instructions are enough to intimidate and I can see a clear reason to do so, I peel tomatoes and remove the seeds. Mostly, however, I couldn't care less for this boring task. What's a bit of tomato skin between friends?

Pitting olives

I know some cooks who are aghast at the idea of buying machine-pitted olives—which does make sense, because they can be too sodden with brine. But life is short, and although I own a pitter and went through a period of assiduously removing every pit before putting an olive in anything, I now either buy pitted olives or use whole ones, and let my guests take their chances. Pitted olives are better if you drain and spin dry them, and coat them in oil before using.

Sifting flour

Bakers will rend their garments at this, but I am no baker; the only cakes I make are deliciously heavy, syrupy brick-like slabs that are barely required to rise a millimetre. The absence of sifting duty is also why almond meal is so appealing.

'Plating'

In a restaurant or other people's homes I can admire the artistry of food presentation, but at home I find it too fussy. I prefer the conviviality, the casual ease, of serving oneself and one's companions from shared platters on the table. It also means you can have seconds.

FIVE VERSATILE DRESSINGS AND SAUCES

Fenella's parsnip cream

Melt butter and sauté 4 large sliced parsnips (remove cores if woody) for 12–15 minutes or until tender. Add 500 ml milk and cook for 5 minutes; season to taste. Leave to cool. Blend or process until smooth, then add 200 ml sour cream and blend again. With motor running, add 100 ml olive oil in a steady stream. Serve warm with lamb or grilled chicken.

Bread and tarragon salsa

Soak a few slices of day-old bread in a couple of tablespoons of red wine vinegar until soft, then whiz in the food processor with a couple of cloves of garlic, the leaves from a small bunch of tarragon, salt and pepper, and add as much olive oil to loosen it as pleases your taste. Serve with slow-cooked lamb, barbecued chicken and roasted meats, or stir through pulses.

Lux's parmesan cream

Boil 3 eggs for 4 minutes, then place in cold water for 1 minute. Meanwhile mash a clove of garlic with 2 drained anchovy fillets and some sea salt, then add 2 teaspoons Dijon mustard, a squeeze of lemon juice, 1 tablespoon red wine vinegar, 2 tablespoons grated parmesan, and stir. Scoop soft eggs from the shell, and blend till creamy in a food processor. With motor running, add the parmesan mix and then, gradually, up to half a cup of olive oil. Taste and adjust seasoning. Serve with rare roast beef.

Herby yoghurt dressing

Combine 250 g natural yoghurt with a tablespoon each of finely chopped dill and coriander, 1 teaspoon honey, and sea salt, mixing thoroughly. Serve with fish, grilled chicken or any salad.

Preserved lemon and garlic dressing

In a mortar and pestle pound a large clove of garlic and a good teaspoon of sea salt. Take one or two segments of preserved lemon and carefully remove as much of the lemon flesh as you can. Discard this, then finely julienne the rind. Combine this with the mashed garlic and some finely chopped parsley or coriander. Toss through green beans, chickpeas or other pulses, or serve with chicken, fish or pork.

FIVE UTENSILS I CAN'T LIVE WITHOUT

Tongs

There are some good cooks I know who don't own tongs. I do not understand how they live. I use tongs for everything from turning roasted vegetables to pulling out bits of pasta to check if it's done to tossing salads to flipping fritters.

Metal skewers

Whenever I stay in a holiday house where there is no metal skewer I go into a near panic—I use them to check the temperature of pies and

LISTS OF FIVE THINGS

quiches, to check if cakes are done, to pierce eggplants for barbecuing and
at a pinch to check the readiness of meat. If you own a holiday house,
I beg you, put a skewer in the drawer.

A meat thermometer
My chef brother-in-law gave me a digital meat thermometer and it
changed my life. Once you know the ideal temperatures of flesh when
cooked, it completely eliminates anxiety about cooking meat.

Long oven mitts
I have so many burn marks on my right forearm a friend once asked
if I had taken to self-harming. Impatience is probably to blame when
yanking pans in and out of a hot oven, but since friends gave me a pair of
oven mitts that reach past the crucial bit of exposed wrist, my injuries are
far less frequent.

Fish tweezers
A specialist item to be sure, but these cost under five dollars and have
made pin-boning salmon quite fun rather than a chore.

277

FIVE GRAINISH THINGS EVERYONE SHOULD KNOW HOW TO COOK

Couscous

Pour 2 cups of couscous onto a baking tray, add the same quantity of warm salted water, mix thoroughly to combine and leave for 10 minutes. Drizzle the couscous lightly all over with olive oil and use your fingers or two forks to lightly fluff the grain, aerating it as much as you can. Allow it to settle in a fairly even layer before covering the pan loosely with foil and putting in a moderate oven for 10–15 minutes until light and very fluffy.

Jane's soft polenta

Combine 4 cups of milk with half an onion, 2 sprigs of thyme and a bay leaf in a heavy saucepan and slowly bring to the boil. Remove from heat and let stand 15 minutes. Remove herbs and onion, return milk to the boil, add half a teaspoon of salt and slowly whisk in 75 g of polenta. Cook over lowest possible heat for about 30 minutes, stirring regularly with a whisk throughout. Add a little boiling water if it becomes too stiff, and season to taste. Serves 4.

Quinoa (yes it's a seed, not a grain, but let's pretend)

Boil a cup of quinoa in 2 cups of water for 12 minutes, then drain thoroughly by spreading over a tea towel to dry. Red and black quinoa take longer to cook than white.

Wild rice

Boil in salted water for 30–45 minutes until the grains are split and it has the nuttiness of texture you like. Drain.

White rice

Warm half a teaspoon of oil in a small saucepan, add 1 cup of rice and swirl, leave on low heat for a few seconds. Add 1¾ cups of just-boiled kettle water and cover with a tight-fitting lid. Bring to the boil, then immediately turn to lowest heat and cook for 8 minutes. Turn off heat and leave, covered, for at least 15 minutes before fluffing to serve. Makes 4 modest servings.

AFTERWORD

It's nearing Christmas as I write this, and the calendar is filling with outings and obligations and deadlines. (This week, alarmingly, these include a commission for a magazine piece which involves me cooking a week's worth of offal. Lying in wait in the fridge is a huge cow's tongue that I am to soak in brine for a day or two and then—I shudder to think of it—*peel* before cooking).

But the weather has finally turned summery, the herb garden is growing wild, the tomato bushes and zucchini vine are bursting with fruit, and all this cheers and reminds me that my life is a lucky one.

Tonight my writing friends are coming to dinner. I have been meeting regularly with a small group of them ever since I seriously began writing more than fifteen years ago. Back then we were just starting to learn. A few books further along, we're still learning—and that's what these evenings together are about. The friendships may have deepened and expanded to include our non-writing lives, our various jobs and partners and households, but these dinners have a particularly sacrosanct quality as we set aside the clamour of the rest of our lives and talk about our work. I think of writing dinners as a still, deep pool of water just off to the side of life's rushing stream, and look forward to the contemplative calm of them every time.

I'm about to sift through the recipe books and see what catches my eye. Writing nights demand simple food; something that can be made in advance and set on the table without fuss. It might be an old favourite—a quick pan-fried piece of salmon with a warm mirin and soy dressing, say, or chicken pieces marinated in rosemary and lemon and thrown in the oven with some chopped potato. Or I could experiment on these friends, testing out a new recipe, as I often do, for they are an adventurous and forgiving lot, and in my cooking life as in my writing life, I am glad to say, there is still so much to learn.

The particular food I make tonight doesn't matter, really. What's important is the fact of eating together—the gathering at the table, the conviviality—and the moment *after* dinner, when plates are pushed aside and glasses refilled, that we can really settle in, and talk. But it's the smell of dinner that greets my friends at the door, and the cooking that creates the space of warmth and welcome, and opens us up to one another.

BIBLIOGRAPHY

Stephanie Alexander, *The Cook's Companion*, Penguin Books, Melbourne, 1996.
Anthimus, *On the Observance of Foods*, trans. Mark Grant, Prospect Books, Devon, 2007.
Gay Bilson, *Plenty: Digressions on Food*, Penguin Books, Melbourne, 2007.
Maggie Beer, *Maggie's Table*, Penguin Books, Melbourne, 2008.
William Boyd, *Any Human Heart*, Penguin Books, London, 2003.
Matthew Brown, 'Picky Eating is a Moral Failing', in Allhof, Fritz & Monroe, Dave (eds), *Food and Philosophy: Eat, Think and Be Merry*, Blackwell Publishing, Malden MA 2007.
NSW Cookery Teachers' Association, *The Commonsense Cookery Book* [full colour cased ed.], Angus & Robertson Publishers Sydney, 1976.
Prudence Crowther (ed.), *Don't Tread on Me: The Selected Letters of SJ Perelman*, Viking Penguin, New York, 1987.
Darmadi-Blackberry, Irene et al. 2004, 'Legumes: The Most Important Dietary Predictor of Survival in Older People of Different Ethnicities', *Asia Pacific Journal of Clinical Nutrition*, 13(2), pp. 217–220.
Elizabeth David, *Italian Food*, Penguin Books, Melbourne, 1977.
Elizabeth David, *A Book of Mediterranean Food*, Penguin Books, Melbourne, 1958.
Annie Dillard, *The Writing Life*, HarperPerennial, New York, 1989.
Joanne Fedler, *When Hungry, Eat*, Allen & Unwin, Sydney, 2010.

MFK Fisher, *The Gastronomical Me* in Fisher, MFK 2004, *The Art of Eating*, Wiley Publishing, New Jersey, 2004.

David Foster Wallace, 'Consider the Lobster', *Gourmet* August 2004, Condé Nast, New York, 2004.

AA Gill, *AA Gill is Away* [ebook], Orion Publishing Group, London, 2010.

Skye Gyngell, *A Year in My Kitchen*, Quadrille Publishing, London, 2006.

Vicki Hastrich, *The Great Arch*, Allen & Unwin, Sydney, 2008.

Lewis Hyde, *The Gift: How the Creative Spirit Transforms the World*, Canongate Books, Edinburgh, 2007.

Jared Ingersoll, *Sharing Plates*, Murdoch Books, Sydney, 2007.

Carolyn Korsemeyer, 'Delightful Delicious Disgusting' in Allhof, Fritz & Monroe, Dave (eds) , *Food and Philosophy: Eat, Think and Be Merry*, Blackwell Publishing, Malden, 2007.

Karen Martini, *Cooking at Home*, Penguin Books, Melbourne, 2008.

Yotam Ottolenghi & Sami Tamimi, *Ottolenghi The Cookbook*, Random House Group, London, 2008.

Neil Perry, *Good Food*, Murdoch Books, Sydney, 2007.

Neil Perry, *Rockpool*, William Heinemann, Melbourne, 1996.

Eduoard de Pomiane, *Cooking with Pomiane*, Serif, London, 2009.

Nani Power, *Feed the Hungry: A Memoir with Recipes*, Simon & Schuster, New York, 2008.

Paul Rozin, Johnathan Haidt and Clark R McCauley, 'Disgust' in Michael Lewis, Jeannette M Haviland-Jones, Lisa Feldman Barrett (eds), *Handbook of Emotions*, Guilford Press, New York, 1993.

Fenella Souter, 'A Voyage Around my Kitchen', *Good Weekend Magazine*, 17 March 2007, Fairfax Media Australia.

Wallace Stegner, *Crossing to Safety*, Penguin Classics, London, 2006.

Michael Steinman, (ed.), *The Element of Lavishness: Letters of Sylvia Townsend Warner & William Maxwell 1938–1978*, Counterpoint, New York, 2001.

Elizabeth Telfer, *Food for Thought: Philosophy and Food* [ebook], Routledge, New York, 2001.

Brenda Walker, *Reading by Moonlight: How Books Saved a Life*, Penguin Books, Melbourne, 2011.

ACKNOWLEDGEMENTS

My sincere thanks:

To the many, many friends and family who have helped me cook, shared their recipes and methods and kitchens and dining tables with me over the years. To the readers of my blog and my Twitter friends who have generously responded to my requests for help, opinions and stories. And to those who (wittingly or otherwise) shared recipes, stories and insights for this book—among them Julie Bail, Caroline Baum, Judith Baum, Georgia Blain, Zoe Bowman, Kate Champion, Stephanie and Silas Clifford-Smith, Zoe Dattner, Tegan Bennett Daylight, Lucinda Dodds, Jane Doepel, Kathryn Elliott, Pat Farey, Janet Grist, Vicki Hastrich, Rebecca Hazel, Lucinda Holdforth, Annette Hughes, Jane Johnson, Tammi Jonas, Michelle de Kretser, Kylie Ladd, Dick Lopes, Anne McElvogue, Bernard Macleod, Alison Manning, Virginia Murdoch, Brian Murphy, Eileen

Naseby, Hannie Rayson, Di Robinson, Peter Simpson, Leslie Solar, Fenella Souter, the Spain family, Louise Swinn, Astrid Turner, Lu and David Wilson, Bernadette, Alice, Louise and Jacqui Wood and families, and Fiona Wood. Thanks also to Charles Such, Manager, Nutrition Services at St Vincent's Health Network for kindly reading the chemotherapy chapter for me, and to Zoe Bowman for her advice on the pastry chapter and her general wit and generosity.

To my brother-in-law and chef, Hamish Pollitt, for firing my culinary enthusiasm over many years with his generous sharing of knowledge, gifts of food, outings, meat thermometers (!) and his fine company, and for reading the manuscript of this book.

To my publisher Jane Palfreyman for her love of life, literature and a good party. To my agent Jenny Darling, who first suggested I write a book on food, and her colleague Donica Bettanin, for their help with the book and for sharing their love of good food with me. To Ali Lavau, for friendship, her excellent cooking, conversation about food and her fine editorial skills, to Janine Flew, and to Siobhán Cantrill and Renee Senogles for their continued care and attention at Allen & Unwin.

To my partner in the kitchen and life, Sean McElvogue, without whom I would have no reason to eat at all.

Last, I would like to thank my late parents, especially my mother, for all the different kinds of nourishment they gave us.

INDEX OF RECIPES

INDEX

RECIPE NOTES

_____

_____

_____

_____

_____

_____

_____

_____

_____

_____

_____

_____

_____

_____

RECIPE NOTES

RECIPE NOTES

RECIPE NOTES

RECIPE NOTES

_____

_____

_____

_____

_____

_____

_____

_____

_____

_____

_____

_____

_____

_____

RECIPE NOTES

RECIPE NOTES

RECIPE NOTES

_____
_____
_____
_____
_____
_____
_____
_____
_____
_____
_____
_____
_____
_____
_____
_____
_____
_____

RECIPE NOTES